The Dance of Life

OTHER BOOKS BY HENRI J.M. NOUWEN
PUBLISHED BY AVE MARIA PRESS

Behold the Beauty of the Lord

Can You Drink The Cup?

Heart Speaks to Heart

In Memoriam

Out of Solitude

With Open Hands

Eternal Seasons, edited by Michael Andrew Ford

The Dance of Life

Weaving Sorrows and Blessings into One Joyful Step

Henri J.M. Nouwen

Edited by
MICHAEL FORD

ave maria press notre dame, indiana

Published by Darton, Longman and Todd, London, UK, 2005

Copyright © 2005 Michael Ford

www.avemariapress.com

ISBN-10 1-59471-087-2

ISBN-13 978-1-59471-087-2

Cover artwork: "The Sower," Vincent VanGogh courtesy of Erich Lessing/Art Resource, NY

Cover and Interior design: Katherine Robinson Coleman

Printed and bound in the United States of America.

Library of Congress Catologing-in-Publication data is available.

TO THE MEMORY OF MY AUNTS,

MARY AND DOROTHY

CONTENTS

STAGE 5: EMOTIONAL HURDLES 113

Stage 6: SPIRITUAL DISORIENTATION 133

Stage 7: INTEGRATING THE SELF 155

Acknowledgments

The author and publishers are grateful for permission to quote copyright material from the following sources:

A Cry for Mercy by Henri J.M. Nouwen © 1981 by Henri J.M. Nouwen. Used by permission of Doubleday, a division of Random House, Inc.

A Letter of Consolation by Henri J.M. Nouwen © 1982 by Henri J.M. Nouwen. Reprinted by permission of HarperCollins Publishers, Inc.

Aging by Henri J.M. Nouwen and Walter J. Gaffney © 1974 by Henri J.M. Nouwen and Walter J. Gaffney. Photos © 1974 by Ron P. Van den Bosch. Used by permission of Doubleday, a division of Random House, Inc.

Behold the Beauty of the Lord by Henri J.M. Nouwen © 1987 by Ave Maria Press, P.O. Box 428, Notre Dame, IN 46556, www.avemariapress.com. Used with permission of the publisher.

Beyond the Mirror by Henri J.M. Nouwen © 1996 by Henri J.M. Nouwen. Used by permission of The Crossroad Publishing Company.

Bread for the Journey by Henri J.M. Nouwen © 1996 by Henri J.M. Nouwen. Reprinted by permission of HarperCollins Publishers, Inc.

Clowning in Rome by Henri J.M. Nouwen © 1979 by Henri J. M. Nouwen. Used by permission

14

THE TERRAIN

This is a book to give you heart on your spiritual journey and I am beginning it in the very house where our internationally renowned guide was born. I am exploring the delightful Dutch city of Nijkerk where a screaming Henri J.M. Nouwen came into the world one winter's day back in the 1930s after a long and difficult delivery. In the years before the Nazi occupation, this was the home of the young Nouwen family. Henri's father, Laurent Jean Marie Nouwen, had moved here to work in the local tax office a short walk away. Today all I can hear is the sound of ticking clocks—the building is now a jeweller's. It prompts me to reflect on something Henri once ruminated on:

> All these concerns about our clock-time come from below. They are based on the presupposition that our chronology is

all we have to live. But looked upon from above, from God's perspective, our clock-time is embedded in the timeless embrace of God. Looked upon from above, our years on earth are not simply *chronos* but *kairos*—another Greek word for time—which is the opportunity to claim for ourselves the love that God offers us from eternity to eternity.[1]

For Nouwen, it was the inner room that mattered most.

Here, with my feet firmly on Dutch soil, I have discovered that a few local residents still remember the Nouwen family. Willem Dirk van Rootselaar, who lives nearby, tells me: "We were a Protestant family and the Nouwens were Catholics. We didn't mix or talk to each other in those days. It wasn't the done thing." His neighbor, Jan van Dasselaar, who worked with Henri's brother, Paul, collects old photographs. He invites me into his home to show me sepia prints of the original Nouwen home which he then reproduces for me on his twenty-first-century computer.

Indeed, my visit here from England is in the finest Nouwen tradition of making prints out of negatives, of seeing dark experiences in a more positive light. The holiday I'd been due to take had to be cancelled at the last minute and disappointment naturally kicked in. That night I didn't sleep well, so I decided to get up and pray in the cold, dark silence of my study. As light dawned, I became distracted and, as my eyes scanned the bookshelves, they came to rest on a map of the Netherlands. As I was about to compile this anthology, I resolved there and then to make an impromptu return trip to Holland, which I got to know quite well during my research for *Wounded Prophet*.[2]

I manage to re-arrange my flights and, within a day, am in the air on a different routing—the sort of restlessness of which Nouwen would have approved. To reach Nijkerk, here in the North West Veluwe region, I fly to Schipol and take a train via Amsterdam and Amersfoort. As I head across the level crossing and into the pedestrianised part of the city (effectively a small town), I have no idea I will be led to the very house where Nouwen was born, although, as I amble through the clean streets, I am naturally curious to know where it might be located. It perhaps would have taken a simple telephone call to find out but, like Henri, I prefer to discover things for myself. My first port of call is the Catholic church of St Catharine, standing on the site of an old building where Henri Jozef Machiel would presumably have been baptised soon after his birth on 24 January 1932. The side entrance is open; standing alone in the passage-way is a solitary wheelchair, a symbol of Nouwen's later ministry. I open the inner door which leads me into a small Marian shrine, separated from the main church by a locked grille. I light a candle for Henri in front of a golden icon of S. Maria de Perpetuo Succursu, adorned with pure white lilies and yellow chrysanthemums.

As I continue my tour, I pass immaculately clean bread shops wafting the aroma of sweet cinnamon, observe Muslim families quietly going about their business and, at the local canal moorings, notice that an animal food ship might well have been named after Henri: it is called Energie. Outside the town hall I spy local children in red and white costumes excitedly forming an arch with their hoops. It transpires they are waiting for their teacher who is about to get married here. Before long, a cream car pulls up and the youngsters serenade the bride with a song they have written themselves.

Keen to find out a little more about the city (which has its own dance school for young and old alike), I speak to a citizen who turns out to be a Calvinist. He has heard of Henri Nouwen but has no idea that he was born in Nijkerk. He tells me that columns of Nouwen's writings are sometimes printed in a newspaper published by the Dutch Reformed tradition. The man directs me inside the council offices. Soon I am learning that the quaint city, which lost half its population in a plague in the same year as its tobacco industry got underway, is the home of a publisher of children's books and is known also for its milk production. More pertinently, I discover that Nijkerk means "New Church" and has its own religious history. In medieval times, a gospel preacher by the name of Ludger built a "God house" on the site of one-time pagan sacrifices, but it was destroyed in a peat fire in 1222, so a new church had to be constructed. That too was consumed by flames in 1540, along with most of the houses. The re-building coincided with the Reformation and the "new church" became Protestant—just the kind of ecumenical roots which would have appealed to Nouwen's sense of communion.

The white bell tower of De Grote Kerk dominates the skyline here. Outside the church I literally bump into a music teacher and campanologist, Niko Poorter, who happens to know exactly where Nouwen was born. Although he is rushing to a lesson, he drives me to the very house. I am amazed to discover that it lies just across the square from the local religious bookshop where ten of Nouwen's titles are on sale. The manager hadn't realized her business was opposite the master's birthplace and beams when she learns the news. Almost every day someone comes in to buy a Nouwen book, she tells me. This would have surprised Henri, who rather suspected that he wasn't really appreciated on native soil. The fruits of his labors share a shelf with the evangelical paperbacks of Adrian Plass. *The Return of the Prodigal Son* is understandably the most popular with his Dutch audience but *With Open Hands, Reaching Out, Here and Now* and *The Inner Voice of Love* are also in demand.

I am not aware that Henri felt any particular attraction to the place of his birth but I think it is always worthwhile to make a simple pilgrimage to the native surroundings of a spiritual guide: to get a feel of the place where a creative spirit came into the world. As I walk in and out of the former Nouwen residence and gain a wider perspective from the other side of the road, I think back to the day when I was in my twenties and was handed my first Nouwen paperback. I later lent that treasured, crinkled copy to a friend who has never forgiven herself for losing it. *Reaching Out,* a spirituality of loneliness and alienation, has helped many on their spiritual journeys. Published when Nouwen was in his early forties, the book was essentially a summa of his theological understanding to date. Years later he maintained it still came closest to his deepest self. At the time it marked a new stage in his writing in that it was crafted largely from his own struggles. In the foreword he notes:

> I wanted to write this book because it is my growing conviction that my life belongs to others just as much as it belongs to myself and that what is experienced as most unique often proves to be most solidly embedded in the common condition of being human.[3]

Although Nouwen's personal style might not have been to everyone's taste, he built his reputation on this semi-confessional approach to spiritual writing. He wasn't an open book, but he was sufficiently transparent to allow others a glimpse into his questing soul. By sharing both the light and the dark sides of his faith, Nouwen connected with a worldwide audience who found both identification and reassurance in his words. The spiritual life, they learned, wasn't necessarily about climbing a ladder of perfection but about embracing one's wounds and finding the transforming power of God at work in them.

Nouwen believed that, in the thick of our anxieties, we can become aware of the various poles between which our lives vacillate and are held in tension. These poles provide a context in which we can discuss the authentic spiritual life. The first polarity, between loneliness and solitude, concerns our relationship with ourselves. During our life we become aware not only of our aching loneliness but also of our real desire for solitude of heart. The second polarity, between hostility and hospitality, is the basis of our relationship with others. We gradually realize that we can be hostile towards our fellow humans instead of being uncon-ditionally hospitable. The third and, for Nouwen, most important polarity, between illusion and prayer, structures our relationship with God.

So often we act as though we are in total control of our own destinies instead of investing in "the precarious gift of prayer hidden in the depth of our innermost self."[4] The spiritual life is therefore a constant movement between the poles of loneliness and solitude, hostility and hospitality, illusion and prayer. The more we come to the painful confession of our loneliness, hostilities, and illusions, the more we are able to see solitude, hospitality, and prayer as part of the vision of our life. So, according to Nouwen, writing about the spiritual life is "like making prints from negatives."[5] He postulates that perhaps it is exactly the experience of loneliness that allows us to describe "the first tentative lines" of solitude. A "shocking confrontation" with the hostile side of our characters might give us words to speak about hospitality as an alternative option. Perhaps, argues Nouwen, we will never find the courage to speak about prayer as a human vocation without "the disturbing discovery of our own illusions."

It is obvious that traditional photographic developers cannot make glossy prints unless they have the dark negatives in front of them. If the negatives are discarded, there can be no pictures. So Nouwen urges us not to bypass loneliness, hostility, and illusion. They are the very route to solitude, hospitality, and prayer. It is in the midst of the old that we encounter new life. The careful and honest articulation (rather than avoidance) of the ambiguities, uncertainties, and painful condition of everyday existence can bring us hope and renewal. Our vision of the future is born out of the sufferings of the present and our compassion for others out of our despair. In other words, only by embracing our shadows can we become fully integrated and authentic spiritual pilgrims. As Nouwen points out.

"Jesus shows, both in his teachings and in his life, that true joy often is hidden in the midst of our sorrow, and that the dance of life finds its beginnings in grief."[6]

After an education with the Jesuits, Henri Nouwen began training for the priesthood in 1950. He wrote his first articles for Catholic newspapers during his seminary years, although he had never planned on becoming an author. He was ordained priest in St Catherine's cathedral, Utrecht, at the age of 25, by Archbishop (later Cardinal) Bernard Alfrink, primate of the Netherlands. He, too, had been born in Nijkerk. Nouwen went on to study clinical psychology at the University of Nijmegen and then, in 1964, left Holland for the United States to study clinical pastoral education at the Menninger Institute at Topeka, Kansas. It was in the late 1960s, when he had taken up a job as a visiting professor in pastoral psychology at the University of Notre Dame that his writing career began almost by accident. After he had given a lecture to a conference of priests, a stringer for the National Catholic Reporter sent the text of his speech to the paper and it was printed in full. Books were soon and frequently to follow throughout his teaching career at Yale and Harvard.

After testing his vocation as a monk and a missionary, Henri Nouwen gave up the academic life in his mid-fifties to become a pastor among women and men with developmental disabilities:

> I'm a very restless person but L'Arche became for me the place where I really came home. There's nothing in me that desires to go anywhere else. I'm still a restless person but in the deeper places of myself I really feel I've found home. In many ways the little ones, the people with limited gifts, have become for me those who have called me home. In their simplicity they reveal for me God's love.

Henri Nouwen was always "on the way home" and he knew fellow sojourners needed sustenance for that journey back into the heart of God. In one of his many articles, he writes that, just as a creative dialogue with other human beings cannot be simply left to our natural responses, so our intimate conversation with God needs formation and training. Nouwen characterises the spiritual life as one in which we struggle from absurd living to obedient living. The word "absurd" is, in fact, derived from the Latin *surdus* meaning "deaf." Absurd living is a way of life in which we remain deaf to the voice which speaks to us in our silence. The many activities in which we might be involved, the many concerns that keep us preoccupied, and the multitude of sounds that surround us make it difficult for us to hear the small voice through which God makes his presence known. Nouwen says that it seems as though the world in which we live "conspires against our hearing that voice and tries to make us absolutely deaf." It is therefore not surprising that we often wonder, in the midst of our personal concerns and obsessions, if anything is actually happening that is worth living for. "Being filled yet unfulfilled, being busy yet bored, being involved yet lonely, these are the symptoms of the absurd life," he comments.

Overcoming our strong resistance to listening in order to become obedient people requires discipline. The three approaches that can help us continually to move away from absurd living to obedient living are the discipline of the Church, the discipline of the Book, and the discipline of the Heart. "These three disciplines can show us clearly what spiritual direction means since all three are connected with the art of becoming listeners to God's voice," he writes.

The Church is the people of God witnessing to the active presence of God in history. It reminds us continually of what is really happening. In the year-round liturgy, the Church unfolds for us the fullness of the Christ-event, as my previous anthology, *Eternal Seasons: A Liturgical Journey with Henri J.M. Nouwen*, attempted to illustrate.[7] The seasons are not simply memories of something that happened long ago, but events which take place in the day-to-day life of the Christian community. In and through the Christ-event of these seasons, God is making his active presence known to us. The more we let the Christ-event inform and form us, the more we will be able to connect our own personal histories with the great story of God's presence in our lives. So, for Nouwen, the Church is always the people of God witnessing to the presence of God in history through the great acts of salvation or the simple commemoration of a saint. This is the first discipline of the spiritual life.[8]

The discipline of the Book or the Bible concerns the practice of meditation. This essentially means letting the word of God descend from our minds into our hearts so that it can enflesh us. Sometimes we may experience difficulty in living a spiritual life because we are too cerebral. The art of spiritual living is to eat the word, digest it, and incorporate it concretely in our lives, says Nouwen. The word of God has to anchor itself in the center of our being. Sometimes liturgical services are verbose. There is not enough silence through which the word can be absorbed in us. Through the regular practice of biblical meditation, we develop an inner ear that allows us to recognize God's word as one that speaks directly to the intimate core of our experience.

Explaining the discipline of the heart, Nouwen points out that praying is not only listening to but listening with. This discipline makes us stand in the presence of God with all we have and all we are: our fears and anxieties, our guilt and shame, our greed and anger, our resentments and jealousies, our questions and doubts, our aspirations and hopes, our dreams and our distractions, our perfectionism and impatience. In short, all that makes us who we are. Nouwen says we have to listen to God's voice and allow God to speak to us in every fiber of our being. This can be difficult because, in our fearfulness or sense of inadequacy, we may feel anxious or want to hide. Perhaps we have become too bored with religion even to bother. Or we may feel estranged from the institutional church for one reason or another. The discipline of the heart means that, wherever we are alone with God, whether in our homes, on a country walk, in the garden, or in a community of faith, we have to own up to our darker motivations, our shadow sides, and bring the parts of ourselves we feel less comfortable with into the presence of the divine. This is true spiritual living. We don't need to grasp the divine. We need the divine to grasp us—just as we are. Henri Nouwen's writings help us do that.

Much has been written about Nouwen's insecurity, yet he sensed inner uncertainty had its own potential for transformation. Moreover, it was a specific vocation for ministers: "Your insecurity, yet be neurotic, but it may also lead to a deep spiritual life." Nouwen felt it was important to find a guide with whom you could feel free to be insecure. He once explained what he meant:

> You're in a big room with a six-inch-wide balance beam in the center. Now the balance beam is only twelve inches off the fully-carpeted floor. Most of us act as if we were blindfolded and trying to walk on that balance beam; we're afraid we'll fall off. But we don't realize we're only twelve inches off the floor. The spiritual director is someone who can push you off that balance

beam and say, "See? It's okay. God still loves you." Take that nervousness about whether you're going to succeed and whether you have enough money—take the whole thing up on that narrow beam and just fall off.[9]

Our guide, who had a number of spiritual directors whom he visited periodically, encourages people to find—and become—soul friends but believes that anyone who acts as a spiritual director should be experienced in the disciplines and familiar with the quiet space where God's voice might be discerned. The way we relate to a spiritual director depends much on our needs, personalities, and circumstances. "It is essential," he advocates, "that one Christian helps another Christian to enter without fear into the presence of God and there to discern God's call." He once told an interviewer:

> A spiritual director is a Christian man or woman who practices the disciplines of the church and of the Bible, and to whom you are willing to be accountable for your life in God. That guidance can happen once a week, once a month, or once a year. It can happen for ten minutes or ten hours. In times of

loneliness or crisis, that person prays for you.

If you are seriously interested in the spiritual life, finding a spiritual director is no problem. Many are standing around waiting to be asked. However, sometimes we don't really want to get rid of our loneliness. There is something in us that wants to do it by ourselves. I constantly see this in my own life.

A spiritual director is not a great guru who has it all together; it's just someone who shares his or her sinful struggles and, by doing so, reveals there is a Presence who is forgiving.

When Nouwen offered a course in spiritual direction, one of the requirements was that students should spend an hour of silence with a selected passage of scripture during his afternoon with them. He would then invite them to come together in small groups to share what they had experienced. Many realized for the first time that something deeper than discussion was happening.

As a clinical psychologist and a spiritual theologian, Nouwen integrates his understanding of the mind with a knowledge of the heart to create books which connect with the core of a person's search for God and the self. He is a bridge between divine revelation and human struggle. Drinking from the wells of his own experience, he builds on the psychologist Carl Rogers' dictum that "what is most personal is most universal." Nouwen discloses his hopes and anxieties with such honesty and intimacy that readers feel he is speaking directly to them. This is what gives his writings credence. He nonetheless acknowledges that "each human being suffers in a way no other human being suffers." Any form of brokenness, though, can be befriended and "put under the blessing." Physical, mental or emotional suffering might be experienced as an intrusion but, according to Nouwen, it can also be claimed as an intimate companion. He explained to me that the spiritual life "is a constant choice to let your negative experiences become an opportunity for conversion and renewal." Human suffering, then, need not be an obstacle to joy and peace, but the very means to it. In a confused and dislocated world, bereft of meaning, Nouwen is a trustworthy companion, even though he admits he does not have all the answers.

But as well as writing to guide others, he writes to discover himself. He uses subjective, relational language which is always welded to an objective, transcendent reference point. The Franciscan preacher Richard Rohr told me that he felt Nouwen was popular in North America because of "his ability to describe inner experiences and outer states." I think that sums it up rather neatly.

Like the fourteenth-century English anchoress Julian of Norwich, Nouwen felt it would profit his fellow Christians if he noted down his experiences. Writing in the late twentieth century, at a time when North Americans seemed more drawn to therapy than religion, his words touched hearts because he understood the depths and the vagaries of human emotions. Moreover, as he had so often "been there" himself, he could write convincingly about searching for God in the darkness of unknowing. In this respect his writings could be said to be mystical, surviving in the great tradition of ascetical theology.

This compilation of Nouwen's writings is intended to guide you through a range of emotional and spiritual issues which might come your way. They are taken from various periods of Nouwen's life and have been re-arranged as though you were setting off on a pilgrimage with him. There are readings to support you as you embark on or renew your spiritual journey, words to inspire you through darkness, loneliness, and inner turmoil, reflections to guide you through periods of difficulty or disorientation, and meditations to help you reintegrate your life and journey towards death, remembering all the while that we always experience the eternal now. Always keep in mind, too, that spiritual journeys cannot be prescribed. We are all individuals and have to go at our own pace.

Grouping the extracts has proved much more testing than the choosing of them because the strands overlap. I hope this selection will enable you not only to identify with the hopes and struggles of the spiritual director's own life but also to make prints out of your own negatives as the next stage of your journey unfolds.

MICHAEL ANDREW FORD
Nijkerk, Holland
September 2004

Notes

1. Henri J.M. Nouwen, *Here and Now: Living in the Spirit* (Darton, Longman and Todd Ltd, 1994), p. 125.

2. Michael Ford, *Wounded Prophet: A Portrait of Henri J.M. Nouwen* (Darton, Longman and Todd Ltd, 1999).

3. Henri J.M. Nouwen, *Reaching Out* (Fount, 1975), p. 16.

4. Ibid., p. 19.

5. Ibid.

6. Nouwen, *Here and Now*, p. 25.

7. Michael Ford, *Eternal Seasons: A Liturgical Journey with Henri Nouwen* (Sorin Books 2004).

8. Ibid.

9. These views on spiritual direction are taken from Richard Foster/Henri Nouwen, "Deepening Our Conversation with God: How to move from monologue to dialogue," reprinted in Leadership, Winter 1997, 112–118.

SETTING

THE

COMPASS

AND ABRAM JOURNEYED ON BY STAGES TOWARDS THE NEGEB. (GENESIS 12:9)

Each Day's Surprise

Each day holds a surprise. But only if we expect it can we see, hear, or feel it when it comes to us. Let's not be afraid to receive each day's surprise, whether it comes to us as sorrow or as joy. It will open a new place in our hearts, a place where we can welcome new friends and celebrate more fully our shared humanity.

BREAD FOR THE JOURNEY

Holy Space

The daily contemplation of the gospel and the attentive repetition of a prayer can both profoundly affect our inner life. Our inner life is like a holy space that needs to be kept in good order and well decorated. Prayer, in whatever form, is the way to make our inner room a place where we can welcome those people who search for God.

After I had spent a few weeks slowly repeating Paul's words, "Love is always patient and kind; love is never jealous—love never seeks its own advantage," these words began to appear on the walls of my inner room much as the license in a doctor's office. This was obviously not an "apparition" but the emergence of an image. This image of a picture with sacred words on the wall of my inner room gave me a new understanding of the relationship between prayer and ministry.

Whenever I meet people during the day, I receive them in my inner room, trusting that the pictures on my walls will guide our meeting.

Over the years, many new pictures have appeared on my inner walls. Some show words, some gestures of blessing, forgiveness, reconciliation, and healing. Many show faces: the faces of Jesus and Mary, the faces of Thérèse of Lisieux and Charles de Foucauld, the faces of Ramakrishna and the Dalai Lama.

It is very important that our inner room has pictures on its walls, pictures that allow those who enter our lives to have something to look at that tells them where they are and where they are invited to go. Without prayer and contemplation, the walls of our inner room will remain barren, and few will be inspired.

HERE AND NOW

Moving into the Unknown

. . . It takes courage to move away from the safe place into the unknown, even when we know that the safe place offers false safety and the unknown promises us a saving intimacy with God. We realize quite well that giving up the familiar and reaching out with open arms towards him who transcends all our mental grasping and clinging makes us very vulnerable. Somewhere we sense that, although holding on to our illusions might lead to a truncated life, the surrender in love leads to the cross. . . .

It is a sign of spiritual maturity when we can give up our illusory self-control and stretch out our hands to God. But it would be just another illusion to believe that reaching out to God will free us from pain and suffering. Often, indeed, it will take us where we rather would not go. But we know that without going there we will not find our life. "Anyone who loses his life. . . will find it" (Matt. 16:25), Jesus says, reminding us that love is purified in pain.

Prayer, therefore, is far from sweet and easy. Being the expression of our greatest love, it does not keep pain away from us. Instead, it makes us suffer more since our love for God is a love for a suffering God and our entering into God's intimacy is an entering into the intimacy where all of human suffering is embraced in divine compassion. To the degree that our prayer has become the prayer of our heart, we will love more and suffer more, we will see more light and more darkness, more grace and more sin, more of God and more of humanity. To the degree that we have descended into our heart and reached out to God from there, solitude can speak to solitude, deep to deep and heart to heart. It is there where love and pain are found together.

REACHING OUT

Leaving Home

For most of my life I have given quite a literal interpretation to Jesus' words: "Leave your father, mother, brothers, sisters for the sake of my name." I thought about these words as a call to move away from one's family, get married, enter a monastery or convent, or go to a faraway country to do missionary work. Although I still feel encouraged and inspired by those who make such a move for the sake of Jesus' name, I am discovering, as I grow older, that there is a deeper meaning to this "leaving."

Lately I have become aware of how much our emotional life is influenced by our relationship with our parents, brothers, and sisters. Quite often this influence is so strong that, even as adults who left our parents years ago, we remain emotionally bound to them. Only recently, I realized that I still wanted to change my father, hoping that he would give me the kind of attention I desired. Recently

43

also, I have seen how the inner lives of so many of my friends are still dominated by feelings of anger, resentment, or disillusionment arising from their family relations. Even when they have not seen their parents for a long time, yes, even when their parents have already died, they still have not truly left home.

All this is very real for those who are becoming aware that they are victims of child abuse. This discovery can suddenly bring the home situation back to mind and heart in an excruciatingly painful way.

In this context, Jesus' call to leave father and mother, brothers and sisters, receives a whole new meaning. Are we able and willing to unhook ourselves from the restraining emotional bonds that prevent us from following our deepest vocation? This is a question with profound implications for our emotional and spiritual well-being.

HERE AND NOW

Portrait of the Self

There can hardly be a better image of caring than that of the artist who brings new life to people by his honest and fearless self-portrait. Rembrandt painted his sixty-three self-portraits

44

not just as "a model for studies in expression" but as "a search for the spiritual through the channel of his innermost personality." Rembrandt felt that he had to enter into his own self, into his dark cellars as well as into his light rooms, if he really wanted to penetrate the mystery of man's interiority. Rembrandt realized that what is most personal is most universal. While growing in age he was more and more able to touch the core of the human experience, in which individuals in their misery can recognize themselves and find "courage and new youth." We will never be able to really care if we are not willing to paint and repaint constantly our self-portrait, not as a morbid self-preoccupation, but as a service to those who are searching for some light in the midst of the darkness.

To care one must offer one's own vulnerable self to others as a source of healing. To care for the aging, therefore, means first of all to enter into close contact with your own aging self, to sense your own time, and to experience the movements of your own life cycle. From this aging self, healing can come forth and others can be invited to cast off the paralyzing fear for their future.

AGING

Spiritual Reading

The great value of spiritual reading is that it helps to give meaning to our lives. Without meaning, human life quickly degenerates. The human person not only wants to live, but also wants to know why to live. Viktor Frankl, the psychiatrist who wrote about his experiences in a German concentration camp during the Second World War, shows convincingly that without meaning in our lives we can't survive long. It is possible to live through many hardships when we believe that there still is someone or something worth living for. Food, drink, shelter, rest, friendship, and many other things are essential for life. But meaning is too!

It is remarkable how much of our life is lived without reflection on its meaning. It is not surprising that so many people are busy but bored! They have many things to do and are always running to get them done, but beneath the hectic activity they often wonder if anything is truly happening. A life that is not reflected upon eventually loses its meaning and becomes boring.

Spiritual reading is a discipline to keep us reflecting on our lives as we live them. When a child is born, friends get married, a parent dies, people revolt, or a nation starves, it's not enough just to know about these things and to celebrate, grieve, or respond as best we can. We have to keep asking ourselves: "What does it all mean? What is God trying to tell us? How are we called to live in the midst of all this?" Without such questions our lives become numb and flat.

But are there any answers? There are, but we will never find them unless we are willing to live the questions first and trust that, as Rilke says, we will, without even noticing it, grow into the answer. When we keep the Bible and our spiritual books in one hand and the newspaper in the other, we will always discover new questions, but we also will discover a way to live them faithfully, trusting that gradually the answer will be revealed to us.

HERE AND NOW

Silent Protection

Abba Tithoes once said: "Pilgrimage means that a man should control his tongue." The expression "To be on pilgrimage is to be silent" ("*peregrinatio est tacere*") expresses the conviction of the Desert Fathers that silence is the best anticipation of the future world. The most frequent argument for silence is simply that words lead to sin. Not speaking, therefore, is the most obvious way to stay away from sin. . . .The central idea underlying these ascetic teachings is that speaking gets us involved in the affairs of the world, and it is very hard to be involved without becoming entangled in and polluted by the world. . . .

This might sound too unworldly to us, but let us at least recognize how often we come out of a conversation, a discussion, a social gathering, or a business meeting with a bad taste in our mouth. How seldom have long talks proved to be good and fruitful? Would not many, if not most, of the words we use be better left unspoken? We speak about the events of the world, but how often do we really change them for the better? We speak about people and their ways, but how often do our words do them or us any good? We speak about our ideas and feelings as if everyone were interested in them, but how often do we really feel understood? We speak a great deal about God and religion, but how often does it bring us or others real insight? Words often leave us with a sense of inner defeat. They can even create a sense of numbness and a feeling of being bogged down in swampy ground. Often they leave us in a slight depression, or in a fog that clouds the window of our mind. In short, words can give us the feeling of having stopped too long at one of the little villages that we pass on our journey, of having been motivated more by curiosity than by service. Words often make us forget that we are pilgrims called to invite others to join us on the journey. *Peregrinatio est tacere.* "To be silent keeps us pilgrims."

THE WAY OF THE HEART

The Inner Debate

O Lord Jesus, your words to your Father were born out of your silence. Lead me into this silence, so that my words may be spoken in your name and thus be fruitful. It is so hard to be silent, silent with my mouth, but even more, silent with my heart. There is so much talking going on within me. It seems that I am always involved in inner debates with myself, my friends, my enemies, my supporters, my opponents, my colleagues, and my rivals. But this inner debate reveals how far my heart is from you. If I were simply to rest at your feet and realize that I belong to you and you alone, I would easily stop arguing with all the real and imagined people around me. These arguments show my insecurity, my fear, my apprehensions. You, O Lord, will give me all the attention I need

49

if I would simply stop talking and start listening to you. I know that in the silence of my heart you will speak to me and show me your love. Give me, O Lord, that silence. Let me be patient and grow slowly into this silence in which I can be with you. Amen.

A CRY FOR MERCY

A House in the Distance

Silence is night
and just as there are nights
with no moon and no stars
when you're all alone
totally alone
when you're cursed
when you become a nothing
which no one needs—
so too there are silences
which are threatening
because there is nothing except the silence.
Even if you open your ears
and your eyes
it keeps going on
without hope or relief.
Night with no light, no hope
I am alone

in my guilt
without forgiveness
without love.
Then, desperately, I go looking for friends
then I walk the streets searching for a body
a sign
a sound
finding nothing.
But there are also nights
with stars
with a full moon
with the light from a house in the distance
and silences which are peaceful and reflective
the noise of a sparrow
in a large empty church
when my heart wants to sing out with joy
when I feel that I'm not alone
when I'm expecting friends
or remember a couple of words
from a poem I read lately
when I lose myself in a Hail Mary
or the sombre voice of a psalm when I am me
and you are you
when we aren't afraid of each other
when we leave all talk to the angel
who brought us the silence
and peace.

WITH OPEN HANDS

STAGE TWO

DISPELLING
THE
DARKNESS

Living in the Shadows

Often we want to be able to see into the future. We say, "How will next year be for me? Where will I be five or ten years from now?" There are no answers to these questions. Mostly we have just enough light to see the next step: what we have to do in the coming hour, or the following day. The art of living is to enjoy what we can see and not complain about what remains in the dark. When we are able to take the next step with the trust that we will have enough light for the step that follows, we can walk through life with joy and be surprised at how far we go. Let's rejoice in the little light we carry and not ask for the great beam that would take all shadows away.

BREAD FOR THE JOURNEY

Negativity

Sometimes we have to "step over" our anger, our jealousy, or our feelings of rejection and move on. The temptation is to get stuck in our negative emotions, poking around in them as if we belong there. Then we become the "offended one," the "forgotten one," or the "discarded one." Yes, we can get attached to these negative identities and even take morbid pleasure in them. It might be good to have a look at these dark feelings and explore where they come from, but there comes a moment to step over them, leave them behind, and travel on.

BREAD FOR THE JOURNEY

Revelation

Perhaps the best definition of revelation is the uncovering of the truth that it is safe to love. The walls of our anxiety, our anguish, our narrowness are broken down and a wide endless horizon is shown. "We have to love, because he loved us first." It is safe to embrace in vulnerability because we both find ourselves in loving hands. It is safe to be available because someone told us that we stand on solid ground. It is safe to surrender because we will not fall into a dark pit but enter a welcoming home. It is safe to be weak because we are surrounded by a creative strength.

To say this and live this is a new way of knowing. We are not surrounded by darkness but by light. He who knows this light will see it. The cripple will walk, the deaf hear, the mute speak, the blind see, and the mountains move. Someone has appeared to us and said: "The sign of love is the sign of weakness: a baby wrapped

in swaddling clothes and lying in a manger."
That is the glory of God, the peace of the world,
and the good will of all men.

I N T I M A C Y

Clouds of Power

The question is: "To what extent are we boss
under our own roof?" First of all, in the
Catholic Church we are very quick to delegate
responsibility but very slow to delegate
authority. Many sermons, lectures, and talks are
aimed at convincing us of the tremendous
responsibility of the priest in the modern world.
But the authority which belongs to this
responsibility is not always a part of the package.
A priest is responsible for the good atmosphere in
the house, but he cannot always change the rules;
responsible for a meaningful liturgy, but he
cannot experiment very much; responsible for
good teaching, but he has to follow the
prescribed sequence of subjects, and especially
responsible for good advice, but he does not feel
free to give his own opinion because he has to
represent someone else's authority instead of his
own. In reality, this means that in a setting of total
institutionalization every sphere of life is
controlled from one central point. This has its

advantages. After all, the general of an army cannot win a war if he has only partial command over his troops or if that command only lasts from 8 in the morning until 5 in the evening. The question for a priest, however, is whether he is really at war.

But there is another, perhaps more complicated, problem. That is the problem of the shadow government. Those who have authority do not always know how much they really have. Often they suffer from lack of clarity. The superior of a house does not know how far he can go because a bishop is watching him somewhere; the bishop does not know how far he can go because the apostolic delegate is looking over his shoulder, and the apostolic delegate is not sure exactly what Rome thinks. The problem is not that some have more authority than others, but that there is no clarity and that the further one gets from the problem, the thicker the clouds become. Perhaps a lot of fear and anxiety about authority is not so much related to power but to the cloudiness of power, which leaves the responsible people always hanging shadowy in the air. Nobody knows who is really saying what and, the further away from home, the vaguer and the more anonymous people become. This is what I mean by the shadow government, which causes this constant referral to eternity, where all lines melt together in a quasi-sacred mystery that cannot be touched.

INTIMACY

Letting Go

Detachment is often understood as letting loose of what is attractive. But it sometimes also requires letting go of what is repulsive. You can indeed become attached to dark forces such as resentment and hatred. As long as you seek retaliation, you cling to your own past. Sometimes it seems as though you might lose yourself along with your revenge and hate—so you stand there with balled-up fists, closed to the other who wants to heal.

WITH OPEN HANDS

Toward the Light

. . . As children of the darkness that rules through fear, self-interest, greed, and power, our great motivators are survival and self-preservation. But as children of the light, who know that perfect love casts out all fear, it becomes possible to give away all that we have for others.

As children of the light, we prepare ourselves to become true martyrs: people who witness with their whole lives to the unlimited love of God. Giving all thus becomes gaining all. Jesus expresses this clearly as he says: "Anyone who loses his life for my sake. . . will save it."

THE RETURN OF THE PRODIGAL SON

Spiritual Combat

Life in community does not keep the darkness away. To the contrary. It seems that the light that attracted me to L'Arche also made me conscious of the darkness in myself. Jealousy, anger, the feeling of being rejected or neglected, the sense of not truly belonging—all of these emerged in the context of a community striving for a life of forgiveness, reconciliation, and healing. Community life has opened me up to the real spiritual combat: the struggle to keep moving towards the light precisely when the darkness is so real.

THE RETURN OF THE PRODIGAL SON

Growing Older

Is aging a way to the darkness or a way to the light? It is not given to anyone to make a final judgment, since the answer can only be brought forth from the center of our being. No one can decide for anyone else how his or her aging shall or should be. It belongs to the greatness of men and women that the meaning of their existence escapes the power of calculations and predictions. Ultimately, it can only be discovered and affirmed in the freedom of the heart. There we are able to decide between segregation and unity, between desolation and hope, between loss of self and a new, recreating vision. Everyone will age and die, but this knowledge has no inherent direction. It can be destructive as well as creative, oppressive as well as liberating.

What seems the most frightening period of life, marked by excommunication and rejection, might turn into the most joyful opportunity. But who is the one who is going to call the elderly from their hiding places? Who is the one who will take their fear away and will lead them out of the darkness of segregation, desolation, and loss of selfhood into the light which is prepared for all the nations to see? Who is the young man who will have the courage to step forward in his society and proclaim that, by ostracising the old men, the traditions will be lost and a series of disasters could take place?

It is the one who cares. Through caring, aging can become the way to the light and offer hope and new life.

_____

AGING

Hidden Joys

I am not accustomed to rejoicing in things that are small, hidden, and scarcely noticed by the people around me. I am generally ready and prepared to receive bad news, to read about wars, violence, and crimes, and to witness conflict and disarray. I always expect my visitors to talk about their problems and pain, their setbacks and disappointments, their depressions and their anguish. Somehow I have become accustomed to living with sadness, and so have lost the eyes to see the joy and the ears to hear the gladness that belongs to God and which is to be found in the hidden corners of the world.

I have a friend who is so deeply connected with God that he can see joy where I expect only sadness. He travels much and meets countless people. When he returns home, I always expect him to tell me about the difficult economic situation of the countries he visited, about the great injustices he heard about, and the pain he has seen. But even though he is very aware of the great upheaval of the world, he seldom speaks of it. When he shares his experiences, he tells about the hidden joys he has discovered. He tells about a man, a woman, or a child who brought him hope and peace. He tells about little groups of people who are faithful to each other in the midst of all the turmoil. He tells about the small wonders of God. At times I realize that I am disappointed because I want to hear "newspaper news," exciting and exhilarating stories that can be talked about among friends. But he never responds to my need for sensationalism. He keeps saying: "I saw something very small and very beautiful, something that gave me much joy."

The father of the prodigal son gives himself totally to the joy that his returning son brings him. I have to learn from that. I have to learn to "steal" all the real joy there is to steal and lift it up for others to see. Yes, I know that not everybody has been converted yet, that there is not yet peace everywhere, that all pain has not yet been taken away, but still, I see people turning and returning home; I hear voices that pray; I notice moments of forgiveness, and I witness many signs of hope. I don't have to wait until all is well, but I can celebrate every little hint of the Kingdom that is at hand.

This is a real discipline. It requires choosing for the light even when there is much darkness to frighten me, choosing for life even when the forces of death are so visible, and choosing for the truth even when I am surrounded with lies. I am tempted to be so impressed by the obvious sadness of the human condition that I no longer claim the joy manifesting itself in many small but very real ways. The reward of choosing joy is joy itself. Living among people with mental disabilities has convinced me of that. There is so much rejection, pain, and woundedness among us, but once you choose to claim the joy hidden in the midst of all suffering, life becomes celebration. Joy never denies the sadness, but transforms it to a fertile soil for more joy.

THE RETURN OF THE PRODIGAL SON

The Possibility of Love

Maybe we remember the few occasions in our life in which we were able to show someone we love our real self: not only our great successes but also our weaknesses and pains, not only our good intentions but also our bitter motives, not

63

only our radiant face but also our dark shadow. It takes a lot of courage, but it might just open a new horizon, a new way of living. It is this breaking through the closed circle, often described as a conversion experience, which may come suddenly and unexpectedly or slowly and gradually. People might call us a crazy idealist, an unrealistic dreamer, a first-class romanticist, but it does not touch us very deeply because we know with a new form of certainty which we had never experienced before that peace, forgiveness, justice, and inner freedom are more than mere words. Conversion is the discovery of the possibility of love.

INTIMACY

Fruitfulness

What is the testimony of the Spirit? The Spirit will witness to the unconditional love of God that became available to us through Jesus. This divine love, as it becomes manifest within the structures of the world, is a light in the darkness. It is a light that the darkness cannot accept. The divine love of God reveals to us that fruitfulness is more important than success, that the love of God is more important than the praise of people, that community is more important than individualism, and compassion more important than competition. In short, the light of the Spirit reveals to us that love conquers all fear. But the world rules by fear. Without fear the world doesn't know how to control or govern.

The Spirit's testimony threatens the world. It is not surprising that anyone who testifies with the Spirit is a danger to the world. That is why Jesus predicts, "An hour is coming when those who kill you will think that by doing so they are offering worship to God. And they will do this because they have not known the Father or me." (John 16:2–3)

These words are very relevant in our days. When we do not live in deep communion with God—that is, with the Spirit of Jesus within us—then religion is easily put into the service of our desire for success, fame, and stardom. From that place we are willing to "kill" whoever is in the way of reaching our goal. The tragedy is that indeed we quickly convince ourselves that we do the killing in God's name.

SABBATICAL JOURNEY

Letting God Be God

One of the greatest challenges of the spiritual life is to receive God's forgiveness. There is something in us humans that keeps us clinging to our sins and prevents us from letting God erase our past and offer us a completely new beginning. Sometimes it even seems as though I want to prove to God that my darkness is too great to overcome. While God wants to restore me to the full dignity of sonship, I keep insisting that I will settle for being a hired servant. But do I truly want to be restored to the full responsibility of the son? Do I truly want to be so totally forgiven that a completely new way of living becomes possible? Do I trust myself and such a radical reclamation? Do I want to break away from my deep-rooted rebellion against God and surrender myself so absolutely to God's love that a new person can emerge? Receiving forgiveness requires a total willingness to let God be God and do all the healing, restoring, and renewing. As long as I want to do even a part of that myself, I end up with partial solutions, such as becoming a hired servant. As a hired servant, I can still keep my distance, still revolt, reject, strike, run away, or complain about my pay. As the beloved son, I have to claim my full dignity and begin preparing myself to become the father.

THE RETURN OF THE PRODIGAL SON

The Divine Touch

O Lord Jesus, you who came to us to show the compassionate love of your Father, make your people know this love with their hearts, minds, and souls. So often we feel lonely, unloved, and lost in this valley of tears. We desire to feel affection, tenderness, care, and compassion, but suffer from inner darkness, emptiness, and numbness. I pray tonight: Come, Lord Jesus, come. Do not just come to our understanding, but enter our hearts—our passions, emotions, and feelings—and reveal your presence to us in our inmost being. As long as you remain absent from that intimate core of our experience, we will keep clinging to people, things, or events to find some warmth, some sense of belonging. Only when you really come, really touch us, set us ablaze with your love, only then will we become free and let go of all false forms of belonging. Without that inner warmth, all our ascetical attempts remain trivial, and we might even get entangled in the complex network of our own good intentions.

O Lord, I pray that your children may come to feel your presence and be immersed in your deep, warm, affective love. And to me, O Lord, your stumbling friend, show your mercy, Amen.

A CRY FOR MERCY

STAGE THREE

GROWING THROUGH ANXIETY

Confronting Compulsions

O Lord, the great spiritual teacher Isaac of Nineveh said: "He who knows his sins is much greater than he who makes someone rise from the dead. He who can really cry one hour about himself is greater than he who teaches the whole world; he who knows his own weakness is greater than he who sees the angels." These words, O Lord, are so true. I realize that my preoccupation with my sinful deeds is a way of avoiding a confrontation with my real sinfulness. An avoidance of a confrontation with my real sinfulness means also an avoidance of a confrontation with your mercy. As long as I have not experienced your mercy I know that I am still running away from my real sin.

Come, Lord. Break through my compulsions, anxieties, fears, and guilt feelings, and let me see my sin and your mercy. Amen.

A CRY FOR MERCY

Moving Houses

How can we live in the midst of a world marked by fear, hatred, and violence, and not be destroyed by it? When Jesus prays to his Father for his disciples he responds to this question by saying:

> I am not asking you to remove them from the world, but to protect them from the evil one. They do not belong to the world any more than I belong to the world. (John 17:15–16)

To live in the world without belonging to the world summarizes the essence of the spiritual life. The spiritual life keeps us aware that our true house is not the house of fear, in which the powers of hatred and violence rule, but the house of love, where God resides.

Hardly a day passes in our lives without our experience of inner or outer fears, anxieties, apprehensions, and preoccupations. These dark powers have pervaded every part of our world to such a degree that we can never fully escape them. Still it is possible not to belong to these powers, not to build our dwelling place among them, but to choose the house of love as our home. This choice is made not just once and for all but by living a spiritual life, praying at all times and thus breathing God's breath. Through the spiritual life we gradually move from the house of fear to the house of love.

BEHOLD THE BEAUTY OF THE LORD

71

Keeping Up Appearances

Often you will catch yourself wanting to receive your loving God by putting on a semblance of beauty, by holding back everything dirty and spoiled, by clearing just a little path that looks proper. But that is a fearful response—forced and artificial. Such a response exhausts you and turns your prayer into torment.

Each time you dare to let go and to surrender one of those many fears, your hand opens a little and your palms spread out in a gesture of receiving. You must be patient, of course, very patient until your hands are completely open.

WITH OPEN HANDS

The Garden for Our Hearts

Solitude is the garden for our hearts which yearn for love. It is the place where our aloneness can bear fruit. It is the home for our restless bodies and anxious minds. Solitude, whether it is connected with a physical space or not, is essential for our spiritual lives. It is not an easy place to be, since we are so insecure and fearful that we are easily distracted by whatever promises immediate satisfaction.

Solitude is not immediately satisfying, because in solitude we meet our demons, our addictions, our feelings of lust and anger, and our immense need for recognition and approval. But if we do not run away, we will meet there also the One who says: "Do not be afraid. I am with you, and I will guide you through the valley of darkness."

Let's keep returning to our solitude.

BREAD FOR THE JOURNEY

Strangers in Our Home

If it is true that in many instances we have become the passive victims of an educational process whose impact on us we can hardly appreciate, it is imperative that we ask what exactly it is that has happened to us. As my first general impression, I suspect that we too often have lost contact with the source of our own existence and have become strangers in our own house. We tend to run around trying to solve the problems of our world while anxiously avoiding confrontation with that reality wherein our problems find their deepest roots: our own selves. In many ways we are like the busy man who walks up to a precious flower and says: "What for God's sake are you doing here? Can't you get busy someway?" and then finds himself unable to understand the flower's response: "I am sorry, sir, but I am just here to be beautiful."

How can we also come to this wisdom of the flower that being is more important than doing? How can we come to a creative contact with the grounding of our own life? Only through a teacher who can lead us to the source of our existence by showing us who we are and, thereby, what we are to do.

. . . We will only be able to be creatively receptive and break through the imprisoning strings of academic conformity when we can squarely face our fundamental human condition and fully experience it as the foundation of all learning in which both students and teachers are involved. It is the experience that teacher and student are both sharing the same reality—that is, they are both naked, powerless, destined to die, and, in the final analysis, totally alone and unable to save each other or anyone else. It is the embarrassing discovery of solidarity in weakness and of a desperate need to be liberated from slavery. It is the confession that they both live in a world filled with unrealities and that they allow themselves to be driven by the most trivial desires and the most distasteful ambitions.

Only if students and teachers are willing to face this painful reality can they free themselves for real learning. For only in the depths of his loneliness, when he has nothing to lose any more and does not cling any longer to life as to an inalienable property, can a man become sensitive to what really is happening in his world and be able to approach it without fear.

CREATIVE MINISTRY

Losing Touch with God

Do you really want to be converted? Are you willing to be transformed? Or do you keep clutching your old ways of life with one hand while with the other you beg people to help you change?

Conversion is certainly not something you can bring about yourself. It is not a question of willpower. You have to trust the inner voice that shows the way. You know that inner voice. You turn to it often. But after you have heard with clarity what you are asked to do, you start raising questions, fabricating objections, and seeking everyone else's opinion. Thus you become entangled in countless often contradictory thoughts, feelings, and ideas and lose touch with the God in you. And you end up dependent on all the people who have gathered around you.

Only by attending constantly to the inner voice can you be converted to a new life of freedom and joy.

THE INNER VOICE OF LOVE

Trust and Freedom

Trust is the basis of life. Without trust, no human being can live. Trapeze artists offer a beautiful image of this. Flyers have to trust their catchers. They can do the most spectacular doubles, triples, or quadruples, but what finally makes their performances spectacular are the catchers who are there for them at the right time in the right place.

Much of our lives is flying. It is wonderful to fly in the air free as a bird, but when God isn't there to catch us, all our flying comes to nothing. Let's trust the Great Catcher.

BREAD FOR THE JOURNEY

Feeling Unwelcome

Not being welcome is your greatest fear. It connects with your birth fear, your fear of not being welcome in this life, and your death fear, your fear of not being welcome in the life after this. It is the deep-seated fear that it would have been better if you had not lived.

Here you are facing the core of the spiritual battle. Are you going to give in to the forces of darkness that say you are not welcome in this life, or can you trust the voice of the One who came not to condemn you but to set you free from fear? You have to choose for life. At every moment you have to decide to trust the voice that says, "I love you. I knit you together in your mother's womb" (Psalm 139:13).

Everything Jesus is saying to you can be summarized in the words "Know that you are welcome." Jesus offers you his own most intimate life with the Father. He wants you to know all he knows and to do all he does. He wants his home to be yours. Yes, he wants to prepare a place for you in his Father's house.

Keep reminding yourself that your feelings of being unwelcome do not come from God and do not tell the truth. The Prince of Darkness wants you to believe that your life is a mistake and that there is no home for you. But every time you allow these thoughts to affect you, you set out on the road of self-destruction. So you have to keep unmasking the lie and think, speak, and act according to the truth that you are very, very welcome.

THE INNER VOICE OF LOVE

Battling with Hostility

The movement from hostility to hospitality is a movement that determines our relationship to other people. We probably will never be free of all our hostilities, and there even may be days and weeks in which our hostile feelings dominate our emotional life to such a degree that the best thing we can do is to keep distance, speak little to others and not write letters, except to ourselves. Sometimes events in our lives breed feelings of bitterness, jealousy, suspicion, and even desires for revenge, which need time to be healed. It is realistic to realize that although we hope to move towards hospitality, life is too complex to expect a one-way direction. But when we make ourselves aware of the hospitality we have enjoyed from others and are grateful for the few moments in which we can create some space ourselves, we may become more sensitive to our inner movements and be more able to affirm an open attitude towards our fellow human beings.

REACHING OUT

A Friendly Emptiness

When we have become sensitive to the painful contours of our hostility we can start identifying the lines of its opposite towards which we are called to move: hospitality. The German word for hospitality is gastfreundschaft which means "friendship for the guest." The Dutch use the word *gastvrijheid* which means "the freedom of the guest." Although this might reflect that the Dutch people find freedom more important than friendship, it definitively shows that hospitality wants to offer friendship without binding the guest and freedom without leaving him alone.

Hospitality, therefore, means primarily the creation of a free space where the stranger can enter and become a friend instead of an enemy. Hospitality is not to change people, but to offer them space where change can take place. It is not to bring men and women over to our side, but to offer freedom not disturbed by dividing lines. It is not to lead our neighbor into a corner where there are no alternatives left, but to open a wide spectrum of options for choice and commitment. It is not an educated intimidation with good books, good stories, and good works, but the liberation of fearful hearts so

79

that words can find roots and bear ample fruit. It is not a method of making our God and our way into the criteria of happiness, but the opening of an opportunity to others to find their God and their way. The paradox of hospitality is that it wants to create emptiness, not a fearful emptiness, but a friendly emptiness where strangers can enter and discover themselves as created free; free to sing their own songs, speak their own languages, dance their own dances; free also to leave and follow their own vocations. Hospitality is not a subtle invitation to adopt the lifestyle of the host, but the gift of a chance for the guest to find his own. . .

To convert hostility into hospitality requires the creation of the friendly empty space where we can reach out to our fellow human beings and invite them to a new relationship. This conversion is an inner event that cannot be manipulated but must develop from within. Just as we cannot force a plant to grow but can take away the weeds and stones which prevent its development, so we cannot force anyone to such a personal and intimate change of heart, but we can offer the space where such a change can take place.

REACHING OUT

Seeking Security

. . . the question is not, "what should I do if I find myself in deep love with another stranger in this world?" but rather, "can this love ever be a reality at all?" Many are asking themselves if we are doomed to remain strangers to each other. Is there a spark of misunderstanding in every intimate encounter, a painful experience of separateness in every attempt to unite, a fearful resistance in every act of surrender? Is there a fatal component of hate in the center of everything we call love?

We probably have wondered in our many lonesome moments if there is one corner in this competitive, demanding world where it is safe to be relaxed, to expose ourselves to someone else, and to give unconditionally. It might be very small and hidden. But if this corner exists, it calls for a search through the complexities of our human relationships in order to find it.

INTIMACY

A Bridge over Troubled Water

Availability is the primary condition for every dialogue that is to lead to a redemptive insight.

A preacher who is not willing to make his understanding of his own faith and doubt, anxiety and hope, fear and joy available as a source of recognition for others can never expect to remove the many obstacles which prevent the Word of God from bearing fruit.

But it is here that we touch precisely upon the spirituality of the preacher himself. In order to be available to others, a man has to be available to himself first of all. And we know how extremely difficult it is to be available to ourselves, to have our own experiences at our disposal. We know how selective our self-understanding really is. If we are optimists, we are apt to remember those events of the day that tend to reinforce our positive outlook on life. If we are pessimists, we might say to ourselves: "Again, another day that proves that I am no good." But where is the realist who is able to allow all his experiences to be his, and to accept his happiness as well as his sadness, his hate as well as his love, as really belonging to his own human experiences? When a man does not have all his experiences at his disposal, he tends to make only those available to others that fit best the image he wants to have of himself and his world. And this is exactly what we call "close-mindedness." It is the blindness of a man to an essential part of his own reality.

A preacher who wants to be a real leader is the man who is able to put the full range of his life-experiences—his experiences in prayer, in conversation, and in his lonely hours—at the disposal of those who ask him to be their preacher. Pastoral care does not mean running around nervously trying to redeem people, to save them at the last moment, or to put them on the right track by a good idea, an intelligent remark, or practical advice. No! Man is redeemed once and for all. Pastoral care means, in the final analysis, offering your own life-experience to your fellow man and, as Paul Simon sings, to lay yourself down like a bridge over troubled water.

I am not saying that you should talk about yourself, your personal worries, your family, your youth, your illnesses or your hang-ups. That has nothing to do with availability. That is only playing a narcissistic game with your own idiosyncrasies. No, I mean that a preacher is called to experience life to such a depth that the meteorologist, the storekeeper, the farmer, and the laborer will all one day or another realize that he is touching places where their own lives also really vibrate, and in this way he allows them to become free to let the Word of God do its redemptive work.

CREATIVE MINISTRY

Creative Weakness

A man can have no greater love than to lay down his life for his friends. (John 15:13)

For me these words summarize the meaning of all Christian ministry . . . There are many people who, through long training, have reached a high level of competence in terms of the understanding of human behavior, but few who are willing to lay down their own lives for others and make their weakness a source of creativity. For many individuals professional training means power. But the minister, who takes off his clothes to wash the feet of his friends, is powerless, and his training and formation are meant to enable him to face his own weakness without fear and make it available to others. It is exactly this creative weakness that gives the ministry its momentum.

. . . Ministry means the ongoing attempt to put one's own search for God, with all the moments of pain and joy, despair and hope, at the disposal of those who want to join this search but do not know how. Therefore, ministry in no way is a privilege. Instead, it is the core of the Christian life. No Christian is a Christian without being a minister.

CREATIVE MINISTRY

The Enemy of Intimacy

Fear is the great enemy of intimacy. Fear makes us run away from each other or cling to each other but does not create true intimacy. When Jesus was arrested in the Garden of Gethsemane, the disciples were overcome by fear and they all "deserted him and ran away" (Matt. 26:56). And after Jesus was crucified they huddled together in a closed room "for fear of the Jews" (John 20:19). Fear makes us move away from each other to a "safe" distance, or move towards each other to a "safe" closeness, but fear does not create the space where true intimacy can exist. Fear does not create a home. It forces us to live alone or in a protective shelter but does not allow us to build an intimate home. Fear conjures either too much distance or too much closeness. Both prevent intimacy from developing.

My own experience with people whom I fear offers plenty of examples. Often I avoid them: I leave the house, move to a corner where I can remain unnoticed, or express myself in flat, non-committal sentences. Sometimes I create a false closeness with them. I talk too long with them, laugh too loudly at their jokes, or agree too soon with their opinions. Whether I create too much distance or too much closeness, I always sense a lack of inner freedom and a resentment towards the power they have over me. . . .

But whether through distance or closeness, fear prevents us from forming an intimate community in which we can grow together, everyone in his or her own way. When fear separates or joins us, we can no longer confess to each other our sins, our brokenness, and our wounds. How, then, can we forgive each other and come to reconciliation? Distance allows us to ignore the other as having no significance in our lives, and closeness offers us an excuse for never expressing or confessing our feelings of being hurt.

IN THE HOUSE OF THE LORD

A Prayer for the Fearful

Today, O Lord, I felt intense fear. My whole being seemed to be invaded by fear. No peace, no rest; just plain fear: fear of mental breakdown, fear of living the wrong life, fear of rejection and condemnation, and fear of you. O Lord, why is it so hard to overcome my fear? Why is it so hard to let your love banish my fear? Only when I worked with my hands for a while did it seem that the intensity of the fear decreased.

I feel so powerless to overcome this fear. Maybe it is your way of asking me to experience some solidarity with the fearful people all over the world: those who are hungry and cold in this harsh winter, those who are threatened by unexpected guerrilla attacks, and those who are hidden in prisons, mental institutions, and hospitals. O Lord, this world is full of fear. Make my fear into a prayer for the fearful. Let that prayer lift up the hearts of others. Perhaps then my darkness can become light for others, and my inner pain a source of healing for others.

You, O Lord, have also known fear. You have been deeply troubled; your sweat and tears were the signs of your fear. Make my fear,

O Lord, part of yours, so that it will lead me not to darkness but to the light, and will give me a new understanding of the hope of your cross. Amen.

A Cry for Mercy

STAGE FOUR

EMBRACING LONELINESS

Making Choices

All human beings are alone. No other person will completely feel like we do, think like we do, act like we do. Each of us is unique, and our aloneness is the other side of our uniqueness. The question is whether we let our aloneness become loneliness or whether we allow it to lead us into solitude. Loneliness is painful; solitude is peaceful. Loneliness makes us cling to others in desperation; solitude allows us to respect others in their uniqueness and create community.

Letting our aloneness grow into solitude and not into loneliness is a lifelong struggle. It requires conscious choices about whom to be with, what to study, how to pray, and when to ask for counsel. But wise choices will help us to find the solitude where our hearts can grow in love.

BREAD FOR THE JOURNEY

Distractions

The roots of loneliness are very deep and cannot be touched by optimistic advertisement, substitute love images, or social togetherness. They find their food in the suspicion that there is no one who cares and offers love without conditions, and no place where we can be vulnerable without being used. The many small rejections of every day—a sarcastic smile, a flippant remark, a brisk denial, or a bitter silence—may all be quite innocent and hardly worth our attention if they did not constantly arouse our basic human fear of being left totally alone with "darkness. . . [as our] one companion left" (Psalm 88).

It is this most basic human loneliness that threatens us and is so hard to face. Too often we will do everything possible to avoid the confrontation with the experience of being alone, and sometimes we are able to create the most ingenious devices to prevent ourselves from being reminded of this condition. Our culture has become most sophisticated in the avoidance of pain, not only our physical pain but our emotional and mental pain as well. We not only bury our dead as if they were still alive, but we also bury our pains as if they were not really there. We have become so used to this state of anesthesia, that we panic when there is nothing or nobody left to distract us. . .

. . . By running away from our loneliness and by trying to distract ourselves with people and special experiences, we do not realistically deal with our human predicament. We are in danger of becoming unhappy people suffering from many unsatisfied cravings and tortured by desires and expectations that never can be fulfilled. Does not all creativity ask for a certain encounter with our loneliness, and does not the fear of this encounter severely limit our possible self expression?

REACHING OUT

A Source of Beauty

We live in a society in which loneliness has become one of the most painful human wounds. The growing competition and rivalry which pervade our lives from birth have created in us an acute awareness of our isolation. This awareness has in turn left many with a heightened anxiety and an intense search for the experience of unity and community. It has also led people to ask anew how love, friendship, brotherhood, and sisterhood can free them from isolation and offer them a sense of intimacy and belonging. . .

But the more I think about loneliness, the more I think that the wound of loneliness is like the Grand Canyon—a deep incision in the surface of our existence which has become an inexhaustible source of beauty and self-understanding. . . The Christian way of life

94

does not take away our loneliness; it protects and cherishes it as a precious gift. Sometimes it seems as if we do everything possible to avoid the painful confrontation with our basic human loneliness, and allow ourselves to be trapped by false gods promising immediate satisfaction and quick relief. But perhaps the painful awareness of loneliness is an invitation to transcend our limitations and look beyond the boundaries of our existence. The awareness of loneliness might be a gift we must protect and guard, because our loneliness reveals to us an inner emptiness that can be destructive when misunderstood, but filled with promise for him who can tolerate its sweet pain.

When we are impatient, when we want to give up our loneliness and try to overcome the separation and incompleteness we feel too soon, we easily relate to our human world with devastating expectations. We ignore what we already know with a deep-seated, intuitive knowledge—that no love or friendship, no intimate embrace or tender kiss, no community, commune or collective, no man or woman, will ever be able to satisfy our desire to be released from our lonely condition. This truth is so disconcerting and painful that we are more prone to play games with our fantasies than to face the truth of our existence. Thus we keep hoping that one day we will find the man who really understands our experiences, the woman who will bring peace to our restless life, the job where we can fulfill, our potential, the book which will explain everything, and the place where we can feel at home. Such false hope leads us to make exhausting demands and prepares us for bitterness and dangerous hostility when we start discovering that nobody, and nothing, can live up to our absolutistic expectations.

THE WOUNDED HEALER

Clinging

I am deeply convinced that gentleness, tenderness, peacefulness, and the inner freedom to move closer to one another, or to withdraw from one another, are nurtured in solitude. Without solitude we begin to cling to each other; we begin to worry about what we think and feel about each other; we quickly become suspicious of one another or irritated with each other; and we begin, often in unconscious ways, to scrutinise each other with a tiring hypersensitivity. Without solitude shallow conflicts easily grow deep and cause painful wounds. Then "talking things out" can become a burdensome obligation and daily life becomes so self-conscious that long-term living together is virtually impossible. . .

With solitude, however, we learn to depend on God, by whom we are called together in love, in whom we can rest, and through whom we can enjoy and trust one another even when our ability to express ourselves to each other is limited. With solitude we are protected against the harmful effects of mutual suspicions, and our words and actions can become joyful expressions of an already existing trust rather than a subtle way of asking for proof of trustworthiness. With solitude we can experience each other as different manifestions of a love that transcends all of us.

CLOWNING IN ROME

Needing Others

Very often [the priest] has lost his private life, where he can be with himself; nor has he a hierarchy of relationships with guards on the thresholds. Being friendly to everybody, he very often has no friends for himself. Always consulting and giving advice, he often has nobody to go to with his own pains and problems. Not finding a real intimate home in his house or rectory, he often rambles through the parish to find people who give him some sense of belonging and some sense of a home. The priest, who is pleading for friends, needs his parishioners more than they need him. Looking for acceptance, he tends to cling to his counselees and depend on his faithful. If he has not found a personal form of intimacy where he can be happy, his parishioners become his needs. He spends long hours with them, more to fulfill his own desires than theirs. In this way he tends to lose the hierarchy of relationships, never feels safe, is always on the alert, and finally finds himself terribly misunderstood and lonesome.

The paradox is that he who has been taught to love everyone, in reality finds himself without any friends; that he who trained himself in mental prayer often is not able to be alone with himself. Having opened himself to every outsider, there is no room left for the insider. The walls of the intimate enclosure of his privacy crumble and there is no place left to be with himself. The priest who has given away so much of himself creates an inexhaustible need to be constantly with others in order to feel that he is a whole person.

INTIMACY

Binding Wounds

The wound of loneliness in the life of the minister hurts all the more since he not only shares in the human condition of isolation but also finds that his professional impact on others is diminishing. The minister is called to speak to the ultimate concerns of life: birth and death, union and separation, love and hate. He has an urgent desire to give meaning to people's lives. But he finds himself standing on the edges of events and only reluctantly admitted to the spot where the decisions are made. . .

The wound of our loneliness is indeed deep. Maybe we had forgotten it, since there were so many distractions. But our failure to change the world with our good intentions and sincere actions, and our undesired displacement to the edges, have made us aware that the wound is still there.

So we see how loneliness is the minister's wound not only because he shares in the human condition, but also because of the unique predicament of his profession. It is this wound which he is called to bind with more care and attention than others usually do. For a deep understanding of his own pain makes it possible for him to convert his weakness into strength and to offer his own experience as a source of healing to those who are often lost in the darkness of their own misunderstood sufferings. This is a very hard call because, for a minister who is committed to forming a community of faith, loneliness is a very painful wound which is easily subject to denial and neglect. But once the pain is accepted and understood, a denial is no longer necessary and ministry can become a healing service.

THE WOUNDED HEALER

Moving into Solitude

The first characteristic of the spiritual life is the continuing movement from loneliness to solitude. Its second equally important characteristic is the movement by which our hostilities can be converted into hospitality. It is there that our changing relationship to our self can be brought to fruition in an ever-changing relationship to our fellow human beings. It is there that our reaching out to our innermost being can lead to a reaching out to the many strangers whom we meet on our way through life. In our world full of strangers, estranged from their own past, culture, and country, from their neighbors, friends, and family, from their deepest self and their God, we witness a painful search for a hospitable place where life

100

can be lived without fear and where community can be found. Although many, we might even say most, strangers in this world become easily the victim of a fearful hostility, it is possible for men and women and obligatory for Christians to offer an open and hospitable space where strangers can cast off their strangeness and become our fellow human beings. The movement from hostility to hospitality is hard and full of difficulties. Our society seems to be increasingly full of fearful, defensive, aggressive people anxiously clinging to their property and inclined to look at their surrounding world with suspicion, always expecting an enemy to suddenly appear, intrude, and do harm. But still—that is our vocation: to convert the *hostis* into a *hospes*, the enemy into a guest and to create the free and fearless space where brotherhood and sisterhood can be formed and fully experienced.

REACHING OUT

Attentive Living

It is probably difficult, if not impossible, to move from loneliness to solitude without any form of withdrawal from a distracting world, and therefore it is understandable that those who seriously try to develop their spiritual life

101

are attracted to places and situations where they can be alone, sometimes for a limited period of time, sometimes more or less permanently. But the solitude that really counts is the solitude of the heart; it is an inner quality or attitude that does not depend on physical isolation. . . A man or woman who has developed this solitude of heart is no longer pulled apart by the most divergent stimuli of the surrounding world but is able to perceive and understand this world from a quiet inner center.

By attentive living we can learn the difference between being present in loneliness and being present in solitude. When you are alone in an office, a house, or an empty waiting room, you can suffer from restless loneliness but also enjoy a quiet solitude. When you are teaching in a classroom, listening to a lecture, watching a movie, or chatting at a "happy hour," you can have the unhappy feeling of loneliness but also the deep contentment of someone who speaks, listens and watches from the tranquil center of his solitude. It is not too difficult to distinguish between the restless and the restful, between the driven and the free, between the lonely and the solitary in our surroundings. When we live with a solitude of heart, we can listen with attention to the words and the worlds of others, but when we are driven by loneliness, we tend to select just those remarks and events that bring immediate satisfaction to our own craving needs.

But what then can we do with our essential aloneness which so often breaks into our consciousness as the experience of a desperate sense of loneliness? What does it mean to say that neither friendship nor love, neither marriage nor community, can take that loneliness away? Sometimes illusions are more liveable than realities, and why not follow our desire to cry out in loneliness and search for someone whom we can embrace and in whose arms our tense body and mind can find a moment of deep rest and enjoy the momentary experience of being understood and accepted? These are hard questions because they come forth out of our wounded hearts, but they have to be listened to even when they lead to a difficult road. This difficult road is the road of conversion, the conversion from loneliness into solitude. Instead of running away from our loneliness and trying to forget or deny it, we have to protect it and turn it into a fruitful solitude. To live a spiritual life we must first find the courage to enter into the desert of our loneliness and to change it by gentle and persistent efforts into a garden of solitude. This

103

requires not only courage but also a strong faith. As hard as it is to believe that the dry desolate desert can yield endless varieties of flowers, it is equally hard to imagine that our loneliness is hiding unknown beauty. The movement from loneliness to solitude, however, is the beginning of any spiritual life because it is the movement from the restless sense to the restful spirit, from the outward-reaching cravings to the inward-reaching search, from the fearful clinging to the fearless play.

REACHING OUT

Being and Worth

A life without a lonely place, that is, a life without a quiet center, easily becomes destructive. When we cling to the results of our actions as our only way of self-identification, then we become possessive and defensive and tend to look at our fellow human beings more as enemies to be kept at a distance than as friends with whom we share the gifts of life.

In solitude we can slowly unmask the illusion of our possessiveness and discover in the center of our own self that we are not what we can conquer, but what is given to us. In solitude we can listen to the voice of him who spoke to us before we could speak a word, who healed us before we could make any gesture to help, who set us free long before we could free others, and who loved us long before we could give love to anyone. It is in this solitude that we discover that being is more important than having, and that we are worth more than the result of our efforts. In solitude we discover that our life is not a possession to be defended, but a gift to be shared. It's there we recognize that the healing words we speak are not just our own, but are given to us; that the love we can express is part of a greater love; and that the new life we bring forth is not a property to cling to, but a gift to be received.

In solitude we become aware that our worth is not the same as our usefulness.

OUT OF SOLITUDE

Vocation in a Lonely Place

. . . The secret of Jesus' ministry is hidden in that lonely place where he went to pray, early in the morning, long before dawn.

In the lonely place Jesus finds the courage to follow God's will and not his own; to speak

God's words and not his own; to do God's work and not his own. He reminds us constantly: "I can do nothing by myself... my aim is to do not my own will, but the will of him who sent me" (John 5:30). And again, "The words I say to you I do not speak as from myself: it is the Father, living in me, who is doing this work" (John 14:10). It is in the lonely place, where Jesus enters into intimacy with the Father, that his ministry is born.

. . . Somewhere we know that, without a lonely place, our lives are in danger. Somewhere we know that, without silence, words lose their meaning, that, without listening, speaking no longer heals, that, without distance, closeness cannot cure. Somewhere we know that, without a lonely place, our actions quickly become empty gestures. The careful balance between silence and words, withdrawal and involvement, distance and closeness, solitude and community, forms the basis of the Christian life and should therefore be the subject of our most personal attention.

OUT OF SOLITUDE

Fluctuation

Our world, however, is not divided between lonely people and solitaries. We constantly fluctuate between those poles and differ from hour to hour, day to day, week to week, and year to year. We must confess that we have only a very limited influence on this fluctuation. Too many known and unknown factors play roles in the balance of our inner life. But when we are able to recognize the poles between which we move and develop a sensitivity for this inner field of tensions, then we no longer have to feel lost and can begin to discern the direction in which we want to move.

The development of this inner sensitivity is the beginning of a spiritual life. . . . By slowly converting our loneliness into a deep solitude, we create that precious space where we can discover the voice telling us about our inner necessity—that is, our vocation.

REACHING OUT

The Virtues of Hospitality

Making one's own wounds a source of healing . . . does not call for a sharing of superficial personal pains but for a constant willingness to

107

see one's own pain and suffering as rising from the depth of the human condition which all men share. . . .

How does healing take place? Many words, such as care and compassion, understanding and forgiveness, fellowship and community, have been used for the healing task of the Christian minister. I like to use the word hospitality, not only because it has such deep roots in the Judaeo-Christian tradition, but also, and primarily, because it gives us more insight into the nature of response to the human condition of loneliness. Hospitality is the virtue which allows us to break through the narrowness of our own fears and to open our houses to the stranger, with the intuition that salvation comes to us in the form of a tired traveller. Hospitality makes anxious disciples into powerful witnesses, makes suspicious owners into generous givers, and makes closed-minded sectarians into interested recipients of new ideas and insights. . . .

. . . Human withdrawal is a very painful and lonely process because it forces us to face directly our own condition in all its beauty as well as misery. When we are not afraid to enter into our own center and to concentrate on the stirrings of our own soul, we come to know that being alive means being loved. This experience tells us that we can only love because we are born out of love, that we can only give because our life is a gift and that we can only make others free because we are set free by him whose heart is greater than ours. When we have found the anchor places for our lives in our own center, we can be free to let others enter into the space created for them and allow them to dance their own dance, sing their own song, and speak their own language without fear. Then our presence is no longer threatening and demanding but inviting and liberating.

The minister who has come to terms with his own loneliness and is at home in his own house is a host who offers hospitality to his guests. He gives them a friendly space where they may feel free to come and go, to be close and distant, to rest and to play, to talk and to be silent, to eat and to fast. The paradox indeed is that hospitality asks for the creation of an empty space where the guest can find his own soul.

Why is this healing ministry? It is healing because it takes away the false illusion that wholeness can be given by one to another. It is healing because it does not take away the loneliness and the pain of another, but invites him to recognize his loneliness on a level where it can be shared. Many people in this life suffer

109

because they are anxiously searching for the man or woman, the event or encounter, which will take their loneliness away. But when they enter a house with real hospitality they soon see that their own wounds must be understood, not as sources of despair and bitterness, but as signs that they have to travel on in obedience to the calling sounds of their own wounds. . . .

A minister is not a doctor whose primary task is to take away pain. Rather, he deepens the pain to a level where it can be shared.

THE WOUNDED HEALER

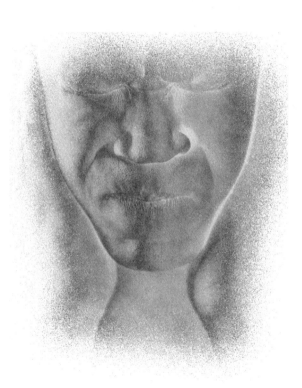

STAGE FIVE

EMOTIONAL

HURDLES

Anger

Anger is indeed one of the main obstacles of the spiritual life. Evagrius writes: "The state of prayer can be aptly described as a habitual state of imperturbable calm." The longer I am here, the more I sense how anger bars my way to God. Today I realized how, especially during work which I do not like much, my mind starts feeding upon hostile feelings. I experience negative feelings towards the one who gives the order, imagine that the people around me don't pay attention to my needs, and think that the work I am doing is not really necessary work but only there to give me something to do. The more my mind broods, the farther away from God and neighbor I move.

Being in a monastery like this helps me to see how the anger is really mine. In other situations there are often enough "good reasons" for being angry, for thinking that others are insensitive, egocentric, or harsh, and in those circumstances my mind easily finds anchor points for its hostility. But here! People couldn't be nicer, more gentle, more considerate. They really are very kind, compassionate people. That leaves little room for projection. In fact, none. It is not he or they, but it is simply me. I am the source of my own

114

anger and no one else. I am here because I want to be here, and no one forces me to do anything I do not want to do. If I am angry and morose, I now have a perfect chance to look at its source, its deepest roots.

THE GENESEE DIARY

Resentment

Resentment and gratitude cannot coexist, since resentment blocks the perception and experience of life as a gift. My resentment tells me that I don't receive what I deserve. It always manifests itself in envy.

Gratitude, however, goes beyond the "mine" and "thine" and claims the truth that all of life is a pure gift. In the past I always thought of gratitude as a spontaneous response to the awareness of gifts received, but now I realize that gratitude can also be lived as a discipline. The discipline of gratitude is the explicit effort to acknowledge that all I am and have is given to me as a gift of love, a gift to be celebrated with joy.

Gratitude as a discipline involves a conscious choice. I can choose to be grateful even when my emotions and feelings are still steeped in hurt and resentment. It is amazing how many occasions present themselves in which I can choose gratitude instead of a complaint. I can choose to be grateful when I am criticized, even when my heart still responds in bitterness. I can choose to speak about goodness and beauty, even when my inner eye still looks for someone to accuse or something to call ugly. I can choose to listen to the voices that forgive and to look at the faces that smile, even while I still hear words of revenge and see grimaces of hatred.

There is always the choice between resentment and gratitude because God has appeared in my darkness, urged me to come home, and declared in a voice filled with affection: "You are with me always, and all I have is yours." Indeed, I can choose to dwell in the darkness in which I stand, point to those who are seemingly better off than I, lament about the many misfortunes that have plagued me in the past, and thereby wrap myself up in my resentment. But I don't have to do this. There is the option to look into the eyes of the one who came out to search for me and see therein that all I am and all I have is pure gift calling for gratitude.

THE RETURN OF THE PRODIGAL SON

Self-Doubt

In this success-oriented world, our lives become more and more dominated by superlatives. We brag about the highest tower, the fastest runner, the tallest man, the longest bridge, and the best student. (In Holland we brag in reverse: we have the smallest town, the narrowest street, the tiniest house, and the most uncomfortable shoes.)

But underneath all our emphasis on successful action, many of us suffer from a deep-seated low self-esteem and are walking around with the constant fear that, someday, someone will unmask the illusion and show that we are not as smart, as good, or as lovable as the world was made to believe. Once in a while someone will confess in an intimate moment, "Everyone thinks I am very quiet and composed, but if only they knew how I really feel. . . " This nagging self-doubt is at the basis of so much depression in the lives of many people who are struggling in our competitive society. Moreover, this corroding fear of the discovery of our weaknesses prevents community and creative sharing. When we have sold our identity to the judges of this world, we are bound to become restless, because of a growing need for affirmation and praise. Indeed we are tempted to become low-hearted because of a constant self-rejection. And we are in serious danger of becoming isolated, since friendship and love are impossible without a mutual vulnerability.

And so, when our actions have become more an expression of fear than of inner freedom, we easily become the prisoners of our self-created illusions.

OUT OF SOLITUDE

Self-Rejection

One of the greatest dangers in the spiritual life is self-rejection. When we say, "If people really knew me, they wouldn't love me," we choose the road towards darkness. Often we are made to believe that self-deprecation is a virtue, called humility. But humility is in reality the opposite of self-deprecation. It is the grateful recognition that we are precious in God's eyes and that all we are is pure gift. To grow beyond self-rejection we must have the courage to listen to the voice calling us God's beloved sons and daughters, and the determination always to live our lives according to this truth.

BREAD FOR THE JOURNEY

Low Self-Esteem

For a very long time I considered low self-esteem to be some kind of virtue. I had been warned so often against pride and conceit that I came to consider it a good thing to deprecate myself. But now I realize that the real sin is to deny God's first love for me, to ignore my original goodness. Because without claiming that first love and that original goodness for myself, I lose touch with my true self and embark on the destructive search among the wrong people and in the wrong places for what can only be found in the house of my Father.

I do not think I am alone in this struggle to claim God's first love and my original goodness. Beneath much human assertiveness, competitiveness, and rivalry; beneath much self-confidence and even arrogance, there is often a very insecure heart, much less sure of itself than outward behavior would lead one to believe. I have often been shocked to discover that men and women with obvious talents and with many rewards for their accomplishments have so many doubts about their own goodness. Instead of experiencing their outward successes as a sign of their inner beauty, they live them as a cover-up for their sense of personal worthlessness.

. . . Many [people] have horrendous stories that offer very plausible reasons for their low self-esteem: stories about parents who were not giving them what they needed, about teachers who mistreated them, about friends who betrayed them, and about a Church which left them out in the cold during a critical moment of their life.

The parable of the prodigal son is a story that speaks about a love that existed before any rejection was possible and that will still be there after all rejections have taken place. It is the first and everlasting love of a God who is Father as well as Mother. It is the fountain of all true human love, even the most limited. Jesus' whole life and preaching had only one aim: to reveal this inexhaustible, unlimited motherly and fatherly love of his God and to show the way to let that love guide every part of our daily lives. In his painting of the father, Rembrandt offers me a glimpse of that love. It is the love that always welcomes home and always wants to celebrate.

THE RETURN OF THE PRODIGAL SON

Painful Memories

How are we healed of our wounding memories? We are healed first of all by letting them be available, by leading them out of the corner of forgetfulness and by remembering them as part of our life stories. What is forgotten is unavailable, and what is unavailable cannot be healed. Max Scheler shows how memory liberates us from the determining power of forgotten painful events. "Remembering," he says, "is the beginning of freedom from the covert power of the remembered thing or occurrence."

If ministers are reminders, their first task is to offer the space in which the wounding memories of the past can be reached and brought back into the light without fear. When the soil is not ploughed, the rain cannot reach the seeds; when the leaves are not raked away, the sun cannot nurture the hidden plants. So also, when our memories remain covered with fear, anxiety or suspicion, the Word of God cannot bear fruit.

THE LIVING REMINDER

Hypocrisy

This morning at the Eucharist we spoke about hypocrisy, an attitude that Jesus criticizes. I realize that institutional life leads to hypocrisy, because we who offer spiritual leadership often find ourselves not living what we are preaching or teaching. It is not easy to avoid hypocrisy completely because, wanting to speak in the name of God, the Church, or the larger community, we find ourselves saying things larger than ourselves. I often call people to a life that I am not fully able to live myself.

I am learning that the best cure for hypocrisy is community. When as a spiritual leader I live close to those I care for, and when I can be criticized in a loving way by my own people and be forgiven for my own shortcomings, then I won't be considered a hypocrite.

Hypocrisy is not so much the result of not living what I preach but much more of not confessing my inability to fully live up to my own words. I need to become a priest who asks forgiveness of my people for my mistakes.

SABBATICAL JOURNEY

Emotional Impulses

It can be discouraging to discover how quickly you lose your inner peace. Someone who happens to enter your life can suddenly create restlessness and anxiety in you. Sometimes this feeling is there before you fully realize it. You thought you were centered; you thought you could trust yourself; you thought you could stay with God. But then someone you do not even know intimately makes you feel insecure. You ask yourself whether you are loved or not, and that stranger becomes the criterion. Thus you start feeling disillusioned by your own reaction.

Don't whip yourself for your lack of spiritual progress. If you do, you will easily be pulled even further away from your center. You will damage yourself and make it more difficult to come home again. It is obviously good not to act on your sudden emotions. But you don't have to repress them, either. You can acknowledge them and let them pass by. In a certain sense, you have to befriend them so that you do not become their victim.

The way to "victory" is not in trying to overcome your dispiriting emotions directly but in building a deeper sense of safety and at-homeness and a more incarnate knowledge that you are deeply loved. Then, little by little, you will stop giving so much power to strangers.

Do not be discouraged. Be sure that God will truly fulfill all your needs. Keep remembering that. It will help you not to expect that fulfillment from people who you already know are incapable of giving it.

THE INNER VOICE OF LOVE

Complexities

Our life is a short time in expectation, a time in which sadness and joy kiss each other at every moment. There is a quality of sadness that pervades all the moments of our life. It seems that there is no such thing as clear-cut pure joy but that, even in the most happy moments of our existence, we sense a tinge of sadness. In every satisfaction, there is an awareness of its limitations. In every success, there is the fear of jealousy. Behind every smile, there is a tear. In every embrace, there is loneliness. In every friendship, distance. And in all forms of light, there is knowledge of surrounding darkness.

Joy and sadness are as close to each other as the splendid colored leaves of a New England fall to the soberness of the barren trees. When you touch the hand of a returning friend, you already know that he will have to leave you again. When you are moved by the quiet vastness of a sun-covered ocean, you miss the friend who cannot see the same. Joy and sadness are born at the same time, both arising from such deep places in your heart that you can't find words to capture your complex emotions.

OUT OF SOLITUDE

Mood Swings

Moods are worth attention. I am discovering during these first weeks in Genesee that I am subject to very different moods, often changing very quickly. Feelings of a depressive fatigue, of low self-esteem, of boredom, feelings also of anger, irritation, and direct hostility, and feelings of gratitude, joy, and excitement—they all can be there, sometimes even during one day.

I have the feeling that these quickly changing moods show how attached I really am to the many things given to me: a friendly gesture, pleasant work, a word of praise, a good book, etc. Little things can quickly change sadness into joy, disgust into contentment, and anger into understanding and compassion.

Somewhere during these weeks I read that sadness is the result of attachment. Detached people are not the easy victims of good or bad events in their surroundings and can experience a certain sense of equilibrium. I have the feeling that this is an important realization for me. When my manual work does not interest me, I become bored, then quickly irritated and sometimes even angry, telling myself that I am wasting my time. When I read a book that fascinates me, I become so involved that the time runs fast, people seem friendly, my stay here worthwhile, and everything one big happy event.

Of course, both "moods" are manifestations of false attachments and show how far I am from any healthy form of "indifference."

THE GENESEE DIARY

Broken Relationships

I am deeply convinced that most human suffering comes from broken relationships. Anger, jealousy, resentment, and feelings of rejection all find their source in conflict between people who yearn for unity, community, and a deep sense of belonging. By claiming the Holy Trinity as home for our relational lives, we claim the truth that God gives us what we most desire and offers us the grace to forgive each other for not being perfect in love.

SABBATICAL JOURNEY

Living Up to Expectations

It is hard for me to concede that this bitter, resentful, angry man might be closer to me in a spiritual way than the lustful younger brother. Yet the more I think about the elder son, the more I recognize myself in him. As the eldest son in my own family, I know well what it feels like to have to be a model son.

I often wonder if it is not especially the elder sons who want to live up to the expectations of their parents and be considered obedient and dutiful. They often want to please. They often fear being a disappointment to their parents. But they often also experience, quite early in life, a certain envy toward their younger brothers and sisters, who seem to be less concerned about pleasing and much freer in "doing their own thing." For me, this was certainly the case. And all my life I have harbored a strange curiosity for the disobedient life that I myself didn't dare to live, but which I saw being lived by many around me. I did all the proper things, mostly complying with the agendas set by the many parental figures in my life—teachers, spiritual directors, bishops, and popes—but at the same time I often wondered why I didn't have the courage to "run away" as the younger son did.

It is strange to say this, but, deep in my heart, I have known the feeling of envy toward the wayward son. It is the emotion that arises when I see my friends having a good time doing all sorts of things that I condemn. I called their behavior reprehensible or even immoral, but at the same time I often wondered why I didn't have the nerve to do some of it or all of it myself. . .

Looking deeply into myself and then around me at the lives of other people, I wonder which does more damage, lust or resentment? There is so much resentment among the "just" and the "righteous." There is so much judgment, condemnation, and prejudice among the "saints." There is so much frozen anger among the people who are so concerned about avoiding "sin."

THE RETURN OF THE PRODIGAL SON

128

Kinship

Every time I take a step in the direction of generosity, I know that I am moving from fear to love. But these steps, certainly at first, are hard to take because there are so many emotions and feelings that hold me back from freely giving. Why should I give energy, time, money, and yes, even attention to someone who has offended me? Why should I share my life with someone who has shown no respect for it? I might be willing to forgive, but to give on top of that!

Still. . . the truth is that, in a spiritual sense, the one who has offended me belongs to my "kin," my "gen." The word "generosity" includes the term "gen" which we also find in the words "gender," "generation," and "generativity." This term, from the Latin *genus* and the Greek *genos*, refers to our being of one kind. Generosity is a giving that comes from the knowledge of that intimate bond. True generosity is acting on the truth—not on the feeling—that those I am asked to forgive are "kinfolk," and belong to my family. And whenever I act this way, that truth will become more visible to me. Generosity creates the family it believes in.

THE RETURN OF THE PRODIGAL SON

The Sea of Love

Dear Lord, today I thought of the words of Vincent van Gogh: "It is true there is an ebb and flow, but the sea remains the sea." You are the sea. Although I experience many ups and downs in my emotions and often feel great shifts and changes in my inner life, you remain the same. Your sameness is not the sameness of a rock, but the sameness of a faithful lover. Out of your love I came to life; by your love I am sustained; and to your love I am always called back. There are days of sadness and days of joy; there are feelings of guilt and feelings of gratitude; there are moments of failure and moments of success; but all of them are embraced by your unwavering love.

My only real temptation is to doubt in your love, to think of myself as beyond the reach of your love, to remove myself from the healing radiance of your love. To do these things is to move into the darkness of despair.

O Lord, sea of love and goodness, let me not fear too much the storms and winds of my daily life, and let me know that there is ebb and flow but that the sea remains the sea. Amen.

A CRY FOR MERCY

STAGE SIX

SPIRITUAL DISORIENTATION

Feeling Off Course

When suddenly you seem to lose all you thought you had gained, do not despair. Your healing is not a straight line. You must expect setbacks and regressions. Don't say to yourself, "All is lost. I have to start all over again." This is not true. What you have gained, you have gained.

Sometimes little things build up and make you lose ground for a moment. Fatigue, a seemingly cold remark, someone's inability to hear you, someone's innocent forgetfulness which feels like rejection—when all these come together, they can make you feel as if you are right back where you started. But try to think about it instead of being pulled off the road for a while. When you return to the road, you return to the place where you left it, not to where you started.

It is important not to dwell on the small moments when you feel pulled away from your progress. Try to return home, to the solid place within you, immediately. Otherwise, these moments start connecting with similar moments, and together they become powerful enough to pull you far away from the road. Try to remain alert to seemingly innocuous distractions. It is easier to return to the road when you are on the shoulder than when you are pulled all the way into a nearby swamp.

In everything, keep trusting that God is with you, that God has given you companions on the journey. Keep returning to the road to freedom.

THE INNER VOICE OF LOVE

Disconnection

While our minds and hearts are filled with many things, and we wonder how we can live up to the expectations imposed upon us by ourselves and others, we have a deep sense of unfulfillment. While busy and worried about many things, we seldom feel truly satisfied, at peace, or at home. A gnawing sense of being unfulfilled underlies our filled lives. . . .

Boredom is a sentiment of disconnectedness. While we are busy with many things, we wonder if what we do makes any real difference. Life presents itself as a random and unconnected series of activities and events over which we have little or no control. To be bored, therefore, does not mean that we have nothing to do, but that we question the value of the things we are so busy doing. The great paradox of our time is that many of us are busy and bored at the same time. While running from one

135

event to the next, we wonder in our innermost selves if anything is really happening. While we can hardly keep up with our many tasks and obligations, we are not so sure that it would make any difference if we did nothing at all. While people keep pushing us in all directions, we doubt if anyone really cares. In short, while our lives are full, we feel unfulfilled. . . .

One way to express the spiritual crisis of our time is to say that most of us have an address but cannot be found there. We know where we belong, but we keep being pulled away in many directions, as if we were still homeless. "All these other things" keep demanding our attention. They lead us so far from home that we eventually forget our true address, that is, the place where we can be addressed.

Jesus responds to this condition of being filled yet unfulfilled, very busy yet unconnected, all over the place yet never at home. He wants to bring us to the place where we belong. But his call to live a spiritual life can only be heard when we are willing honestly to confess our own homeless and worrying existence and recognize its fragmenting effect on our daily life. Only then can a desire for our true home develop. It is of this desire that Jesus speaks when he says, "Do not worry. . . Set your hearts on his kingdom first. . . and all these other things will be given you as well."

MAKING ALL THINGS NEW

Losing Heart

If you view your weakness as a disgrace, you will come to rely on prayer only in extreme need and come to consider prayer as a forced confession of your impotence. But if you see your weakness as that which makes you worth loving, and if you are always prepared to be surprised at the power the other gives you, you will discover through praying that living means living together.

A prayer that makes you lose heart can hardly be called a prayer. For you will lose heart when you presume that you must be able to do everything yourself, that every gift to you from the other is a proof of your inferiority and that you are a full person only when you no longer have any need of the other.

But with this mindset you become weary and exhausted from your efforts to prove you can do it alone, and every failure becomes cause for shame. You lose your buoyancy and become bitter. You conclude that other people are enemies and rivals who have outwitted you. Thus you condemn yourself to loneliness because you perceive every hand which reaches out to you as a threat to your sense of honor.

When God asked Adam, "Where are you?" Adam answered, "I was hiding" (Gen. 3:9–10). He confessed his true condition. This confession opened him to God. When we pray, we come out of our shelters and not only see our own nakedness but also see that there is no enemy to hide from, only a friend who likes nothing better than to clothe us with a new coat. Certainly praying takes some admissions. It requires the humble recognition of our condition as broken human beings. However, prayer does not lead us to shame, guilt, or despair but rather to the joyful discovery that we are only human and that God is truly God.

WITH OPEN HANDS

Displacement

The paradox of the Christian community is that people are gathered together in voluntary displacement. The togetherness of those who form a Christian community is a being-gathered-in-displacement. According to Webster's dictionary, displacement means "to move or to shift from the ordinary or proper place." This becomes a telling definition when we realize the extent to which we are preoccupied with adapting ourselves to the prevalent norms and values of our milieu. . . .

. . .In voluntary displacement, we cast off the illusion of "having it together" and thus begin to experience our true condition, which is that we, like everyone else, are pilgrims on the way, sinners in need of grace. Through voluntary displacement, we counteract the tendency to become settled in a false comfort and to forget the fundamentally unsettled position that we share with all people. Voluntary displacement leads us to the existential recognition of our inner brokenness and thus brings us to a deeper solidarity with the brokenness of our fellow human beings. Community, as the place of compassion, therefore always requires displacement. The Greek word for church, ekklesia—from *ek* = out, and *kaleo* = call— indicates that, as a Christian community, we are people who together are called out of our familiar places to unknown territories, out of our ordinary and proper places to the places where people hurt and where we can experience with them our common human brokenness and our common need for healing.

COMPASSION

139

The Humility of God

Voluntary displacement as a way of life rather than as a unique event is the mark of discipleship. The Lord, whose compassion we want to manifest in time and place, is indeed the displaced Lord. Paul describes Jesus as the one who voluntarily displaced himself. "His state was divine, yet he did not cling to his equality with God but emptied himself to assume the condition of a slave, and became as we are" (Phil. 2:6–7). A greater displacement cannot be conceived. The mystery of the incarnation is that God did not remain in the place that was proper for him but moved to the condition of a suffering human being. God gave up his heavenly place and took a humble place among mortal men and women. God displaced himself so that nothing human would be alien to him and he could experience fully the brokenness of our human condition.

COMPASSION

Alienation

. . .[Thomas Merton's] writing became an entrance to real silence and solitude. Writing in fact became for him the only way to sanctity. "If I am to be a saint," he writes, "I must also put down on paper what I have become. . . to put myself down on paper. . . with the most complete simplicity and integrity, masking nothing. . ." (The Sign of Jesus, pp. 288–9).

In his work as a writer, Merton discovered also a new experience of poverty. By his writing he had made himself and his most inner feelings and thoughts a public possession. In this way he had disowned himself and allowed others to enter his monastic silence. In this way his fame had made him spiritually poor. But this same poverty made the world around him appear to him in a new way. It seems as if everything belonged to him just when there was nothing left to him which he could call his "private property." The air, the trees, the whole world, were now singing the honor of God and he felt fire and music in the earth under his feet. The beauty of creation made him poor and wealthy at the same time and gave him peace and happiness. This beauty kept him from wanting to experience nature as a possession, but helped him to deeply experience his silence and solitude.

But this solitude and rest were cruelly disturbed during a period of terrible anxiety and uncertainty. In December 1949, Merton wrote, desperate as a sick and depressed person who has just lost his orientation and feels completely alienated from himself: "It is fear that is driving me into solitude" (SOJ, p. 248). It seemed as if everything were broken to pieces and as if nothing were left of the beautiful contemplative ideals. "I am exhausted by fear," (SOJ, p. 248) he wrote. After eight years of life in the monastery, he felt miserable, sinful, guilty and without any prospects. The solitude was now felt as harsh, difficult and painful and gave him the experience of being empty and even totally "nothing."

But then, at the depth of his misery, he again found God and his fellow human beings. When everything was dark, he found himself in God's own solitude.

THOMAS MERTON: CONTEMPLATIVE CRITIC

Comparing Ourselves with Others

Often we want to be somewhere other than where we are, or even to be someone other than who we are. We tend to compare ourselves constantly with others and wonder why we are not as rich, as intelligent, as simple, as generous or as saintly as they are. Such comparisons make us feel guilty, ashamed, or jealous. It is very important to realize that our vocation is hidden in where we are and who we are. We are unique human beings, each with a call to realize in life what nobody else can, and to realize it in the concrete context of the here and now.

We will never find our vocations by trying to figure out whether we are better or worse than others. We are good enough to do what we are called to do. Be yourself!

BREAD FOR THE JOURNEY

Identity Crisis

Being back in France makes me think much about countries and cultures. During the past few months I have been in Holland, Germany, Canada, the United States, and England, and in all these countries I have had intense contact with people and their ways of living, praying, and playing.

There is a great temptation to want to know which culture is the best and where I am most happy and at home. But this way of thinking leads to endless frustrations because the Dutch, Germans, the French, the Americans, and the

Canadians are all people who have unique ways of feeling, thinking, and behaving, none of which totally fits my needs, but all of which have gifts for me.

I know people who complain about the Germans while in Germany and about the Americans while in America, moving themselves and their families back and forth, always wondering what the best place is to live without ever being truly content. Some people, then, are always disappointed with someone or something. They complain about the rigidity of the German Church and the sloppiness of the American Church. Or they may complain about the critical attitude of the Dutch, the mystical attitude of the French, the pragmatic attitude of the Americans, and the formalistic attitude of the English, while never really worshipping deeply at any one place.

I am increasingly aware of how important it is to enjoy what is given and to fully live where one is. If I could just fully appreciate the need for independence of the Dutch, the spiritual visions of the French, the concreteness of the Americans, the theological concepts of the Germans, and the sense of ceremony of the English, I could come to learn much about life everywhere and truly become present to where I am, always growing deeper in the spirit of gratitude.

144

Do we really need to belong to one country or one culture? In our world, where distances are becoming less each day, it seems important to become less and less dependent on one place, one language, one culture, or one style of life, but to experience oneself as a member of the human family, belonging to God and free to be wherever we are called to be. I even wonder if the ability to be in so many places so quickly and so often is not an invitation to grow deeper in the spirit and let our identity be more rooted in God and less in the place in which we happen to be.

THE ROAD TO DAYBREAK

Homelessness

Probably no word better summarizes the suffering of our times than the word "homeless." It reveals one of our deepest and most painful conditions, the condition of not having a sense of belonging, of not having a place where we can feel safe, cared for, protected, and loved.

The first and most obvious quality of a home is its intimacy. When we say: "I do not feel at home here" we express an uneasiness that does not permit intimacy. When we say: "I wish I were home" we express a longing for that intimate place that offers us a sense of belonging. Even though many people suffer much from conflicts at home, even though much emotional suffering finds its roots at home, and even though "broken homes" are increasingly blamed for crimes and illnesses, the word "home" continues to carry with it a warm love and remains one of the most evocative symbols for happiness. The Christian faith even calls us to experience life as "going home" and death as "coming home at last."

IN THE HOUSE OF THE LORD

Lost Self

I am beginning now to see how radically the character of my spiritual journey will change when I no longer think of God as hiding out and making it as difficult as possible for me to find him, but, instead, as the one who is looking for me while I am doing the hiding. When I look through God's eyes at my lost self and discover God's joy at my coming home, then my life may become less anguished and more trusting.

Wouldn't it be good to increase God's joy by letting God find me and carry me home and celebrate my return with the angels? Wouldn't it be wonderful to make God smile by giving God the chance to find me and love me lavishly? Questions like these raise a real issue: that of my own self-concept. Can I accept that I am worth looking for? Do I believe that there is a real desire in God to simply be with me?

THE RETURN OF THE PRODIGAL SON

A Fragile Shelter

How often is the intimate encounter of two persons an expression of their total freedom? Many people are driven into each other's arms in fear and trembling. They embrace each other in despair and loneliness. They cling to each other to prevent worse things from happening. Their sleep together is only an expression of their desire to escape the threatening world, to forget their deep frustration, to ease for a minute the unbearable tension of a demanding society, to experience some warmth, protection, and safety. Their privacy does not create a place where they both can grow in freedom and share their mutual discoveries, but a fragile shelter in a stormy world.

INTIMACY

Illusion and Reality

The greatest obstacle to our entering into that profound dimension of life, where our prayer takes place, is our all-pervasive illusion of immortality. At first it seems unlikely or simply untrue that we have such an illusion, since on many levels we are quite aware of our mortality . . . Although we keep telling each other and ourselves that we will not live forever and that we are going to die soon, our daily actions, thoughts and concerns keep revealing to us how hard it is to fully accept the reality of our own statements.

Small, seemingly innocent events keep telling us how easily we eternalize ourselves and our world. It takes only a hostile word to make us feel sad and lonely. It takes only a rejecting gesture to plunge us into self-complaint. It takes only a substantial failure in our work to lead us into a self-destructive depression. Although we have learned from parents, teachers, friends, and many books, sacred as well as profane, that we are worth more than what the world makes us, we keep giving an eternal value to the things we own, the people we know, the plans we have, and the successes we "collect." Indeed, it takes only a small disruption to lay our illusion of immortality bare and to reveal how much we have become victimised by our surrounding world suggesting to us that we are "in control." Aren't the many feelings of sadness, heaviness of heart, and even dark despair often intimately connected with the exaggerated seriousness with which we have clothed the people we know, the ideas to which we are exposed, and the events we are part of? This lack of distance, which excludes the humor in life, can create a suffocating depression which prevents us from lifting our heads above the horizon of our own limited existence.

REACHING OUT

The Death of Prayer

The truth is that I do not feel much, if anything, when I pray. There are no warm emotions, bodily sensations, or mental visions. None of my five senses is being touched—no special smells, no special sounds, so special sights, no special tastes, and no special movements. Whereas for a long time the Spirit acted so clearly through my flesh, now I feel nothing. I have lived with the expectation that prayer would become easier as I grow older and closer to death. But the opposite seems to be happening. The words darkness and dryness seem to best describe my prayer today.

Maybe part of this darkness and dryness is the result of my overactivity. As I grow older I become busier and spend less and less time in prayer. But I probably should not blame myself in that way. The real questions are: "What are the darkness and the dryness about? What do they call me to?" Responding to these questions might well be the main task of my sabbatical. I know that Jesus, at the end of his life, felt abandoned by God. "My God, my God," he cried out on the cross, "why have you forsaken me?" (Matt. 27:46). His body had been destroyed by his torturers, his mind was no longer able to grasp the meaning of his existence, and his soul was void of any consolation. Still, it was from his broken heart that water and blood, signs of new life, came out.

Are the darkness and dryness of my prayer signs of God's absence, or are they signs of a presence deeper and wider than my senses can contain? Is the death of my prayer the end of my intimacy with God or the beginning of a new communion, beyond words, emotions, and bodily sensations?

SABBATICAL JOURNEY

Soul Work

Prayer is the bridge between our conscious and unconscious lives. Often there is a large abyss between our thoughts, words, and actions, and the many images that emerge in our daydreams and night dreams. To pray is to connect these two sides of our lives by going to the place where God dwells. Prayer is "soul work" because our souls are those sacred centers where all is one and where God is with us in the most intimate way. Thus we must pray without ceasing so that we can become truly whole and holy.

BREAD FOR THE JOURNEY

Dangerous Prayer

Praying is no easy matter. It demands a relationship in which you allow someone other than yourself to enter into the very center of your person, to see there what you would rather leave in darkness, and to touch there what you would rather leave untouched. Why would you really want to do that? Perhaps you would let the other cross your inner threshold to see something or to touch something, but to allow the other into that place where your intimate life is shaped—that is dangerous and calls for defense.

WITH OPEN HANDS

A Prayer in Distraction

Why, O Lord, is it so hard for me to keep my heart directed towards you? Why do the many little things I want to do, and the many people I know, keep crowding my mind, even during the hours that I am totally free to be with you and you alone? Why does my mind wander off in so many directions, and why does my heart desire the things that lead me astray? Are you not enough for me? Do I keep doubting your love and care, your mercy and grace? Do I keep wondering, in the center of my being, whether you will give me all I need if I just keep my eyes on you?

Please accept my distractions, my fatigue, my irritations, and my faithless wanderings. You know me more deeply and fully than I know myself. You love me with a greater love than I can love myself. You even offer me more than I can desire. Look at me, see me in all my misery and inner confusion, and let me sense your presence in the midst of my turmoil. All I can do is show myself to you. Yet, I am afraid to do so. I am afraid that you will reject me. But I know—with the knowledge of faith—that you desire to give me your love. The only thing you ask of me is not to hide from you, not to run away in despair, not to act as if you were a relentless despot.

Take my tired body, my confused mind, and my restless soul into your arms and give me rest, simple quiet rest. Do I ask too much too soon? I should not worry about that. You will let me know. Come, Lord Jesus, come. Amen.

A CRY FOR MERCY

INTEGRATING
THE SELF

Spiritual Maturity

There is within you a lamb and a lion. Spiritual maturity is the ability to let lamb and lion lie down together. Your lion is your adult, aggressive self. It is your initiative-taking and decision-making self. But there is also your fearful, vulnerable lamb, the part of you that needs affection, support, affirmation, and nurturing.

When you heed only your lion, you will find yourself overextended and exhausted. When you take notice only of your lamb, you will easily become a victim of your need for other people's attention. The art of spiritual living is to fully claim both your lion and your lamb. Then you can act assertively without denying your own needs. And you can ask for affection and care without betraying your talent to offer leadership.

Developing your identity as a child of God in no way means giving up your responsibilities. Likewise, claiming your adult self in no way means that you cannot become increasingly a child of God. In fact, the opposite is true. The more you can feel safe as a child of God, the freer you will be to claim your mission in the world as a responsible human being. And the more you claim that you have a unique task to fulfill for

God, the more open you will be to letting your deepest need be met.

The kingdom of peace that Jesus came to establish begins when your lion and your lamb can freely and fearlessly lie down together.

THE INNER VOICE OF LOVE

The Prayer of the Heart

The Desert Fathers in their sayings point us towards a very holistic view of prayer. They pull us away from our intellectualizing practices, in which God becomes one of the many problems we have to address. They show us that real prayer penetrates to the marrow of our soul and leaves nothing untouched. The prayer of the heart is a prayer that does not allow us to limit our relationship with God to interesting words or pious emotions. By its very nature such prayer transforms our whole being into Christ precisely because it opens the eyes of our soul to the truth of ourselves as well as to the truth of God. In our heart we come to see ourselves as sinners embraced by the mercy of God. It is this vision that makes us cry out, "Lord Jesus Christ, Son of the living God, have mercy on me, a sinner." The prayer of the heart challenges us to hide absolutely nothing from God and to surrender ourselves unconditionally to his mercy.

Thus the prayer of the heart is the prayer of truth. It unmasks the many illusions about ourselves and about God and leads us into the true relationship of the sinner to the merciful God. This truth is what gives us the "rest" of the *hesychast*. To the degree that this truth anchors itself in our heart, we will be less distracted by worldly thoughts and more single-mindedly directed towards the Lord of both our hearts and the universe. Thus the words of Jesus, "Happy the pure in heart: they shall see God" (Matt. 5:8), will become real in our prayer. Temptations and struggles will remain to the end of our lives, but with a pure heart we will be restful even in the midst of a restless existence.

THE WAY OF THE HEART

Seeing Wisely

Acting, speaking, and even reflective thinking may at times be too demanding, but we are forever seeing. When we dream, we see. When we stare in front of us, we see. When we close our eyes to rest, we see. We see trees, houses, roads and cars, seas and mountains, animals and people, places and faces, shapes and colors. We see clearly or vaguely, but always we find something to see.

But what do we really choose to see? It makes a great difference whether we see a flower or a snake, a gentle smile or menacing teeth, a dancing couple or a hostile crowd. We do have a choice. Just as we are responsible for what we eat, so we are responsible for what we see. It is easy to become a victim of the vast array of visual stimuli surrounding us. The "powers and principalities" control many of our daily images. Posters, billboards, television, videocassettes, movies, and store windows continuously assault our eyes and inscribe their images upon our memories.

Still we do not have to be passive victims of a world that wants to entertain and distract us. We can make some decisions and choices. A spiritual life in the midst of our energy-draining society requires us to take conscious steps to safeguard that inner space where we can keep our eyes fixed on the beauty of the Lord.

BEHOLD THE BEAUTY OF THE LORD

Acceptance

You become a person only when you are capable of standing open to all the gifts which are prepared for you.

Giving can easily become a means of manipulation where the one who receives a gift becomes dependent on the will of the one who gives it.

When you give, you are the master of the situation, you can dole out the goods to those you think deserving. You have control over your milieu, and you can enjoy the power your possessions give you.

Acceptance is something else. When we accept a gift, we invite others into our world and are ready to give them a place in our own lives. If we give gifts to our friends, we expect them to give them a place in their home. Ultimately, gifts become gifts only when they are accepted. When gifts are accepted, they acquire a place in the life of the receiver. It is understandable that many people want to give a gift in return as soon as possible, thereby re-establishing the balance and getting rid of any dependent relationship. We often see more trading than accepting. Many of us are even embarrassed with a present because we know not how to reciprocate. "It makes me feel obligated," we often say.

Perhaps the challenge of the gospel lies precisely in the invitation to accept a gift for which we can give nothing in return. For the gift is the life breath of God, the Spirit poured out on us through Jesus Christ. This life breath frees us from fear and gives us new room to live . . . When we live from God's breath we can recognize with joy that the same breath that keeps us alive is also the source of life for our brothers and sisters. This realization makes our fear of the other disappear, our weapons fall away, and brings a smile to our lips. When we recognize the breath of God in others, we can let them enter our life and receive the gifts they offer us.

WITH OPEN HANDS

Separation and Communion

A desire for communion has been part of you since you were born. The pain of separation, which you experienced as a child and continue to experience now, reveals to you this deep hunger. All your life you have searched for a communion that would break your fear of death. This desire is sincere. Don't look on it as

161

an expression of your neediness or as a symptom of your neurosis. It comes from God and is part of your true vocation.

Nonetheless, your fear of abandonment and rejection is so intense that your search for communion is often replaced by a longing for concrete expression of friendship or affection. You want deep communion, but you end up looking for invitations, letters, phone calls, gifts, and similar gestures. When these do not come in the way you wish, you start distrusting even your deep desire for communion. Your search for communion often takes place too far from where true communion can be found.

Still, communion is your authentic desire, and it will be given to you. But you have to dare to stop seeking gifts and favors like a petulant child and trust that your deepest longing will be fulfilled. Dare to lose your life and you will find it. Trust in Jesus' words: "There is no one who has left house, brothers, sisters, mother, father, children or land for my sake and for the sake of the gospel who will not receive a hundred times as much, houses, brothers, sisters, mothers, children and land—and persecutions too—now in this present time and, in the world to come, eternal life" (Mark 10:29–30).

The Dance of Life

In the world about us, a radical distinction is made between joy and sorrow. People tend to say: "When you are glad, you cannot be sad, and when you are sad, you cannot be glad." In fact, our contemporary society does everything possible to keep sadness and gladness separated. Sorrow and pain must be kept away at all cost because they are the opposites of the gladness and happiness we desire.

Death, illness, human brokenness. . .all have to be hidden from our sight because they keep us from the happiness for which we strive. They are obstructions on our way to the goal of life.

The vision offered by Jesus stands in sharp contrast to this worldly vision. Jesus shows, both in his teachings and in his life, that true joy often is hidden in the midst of our sorrow, and that the dance of life finds its beginnings in grief. He says: "Unless the grain of wheat dies, it cannot bear fruit. . . Unless we lose our lives, we cannot find them; unless the Son of Man dies, he cannot send the Spirit." To his two disciples who were dejected after his suffering and death, Jesus says: "You foolish people, so slow to believe all that the prophets have said!

Was it not necessary that Christ should suffer and so enter into his glory?"

Here a completely new way of living is revealed. It is the way in which pain can be embraced, not out of a desire to suffer, but in the knowledge that something new will be born in the pain. Jesus calls our pains "labor pains." He says: "A woman in childbirth suffers because her time has come; but when she has given birth to the child, she forgets the suffering in her joy that a human being has been born into the world" (John 16:21).

The cross has become the most powerful symbol of this new vision. The cross is a symbol of death and of life, of suffering and of joy, of defeat and of victory. It's the cross that shows us the way.

HERE AND NOW

The Movements

If God is found in our hard times, then all of life, no matter how apparently insignificant or difficult, can open us to God's work among us. To be grateful does not mean repressing our remembered hurts. But as we come to God with our hurts—honestly, not superficially—

something life changing can begin slowly to happen. We discover how God is the One who invites us to healing. We realize that any dance of celebration must weave both the sorrows and the blessings into a joyful step.

. . .The mystery of the dance is that its movements are discovered in the mourning. To heal is to let the Holy Spirit call me to dance, to believe again, even amid my pain, that God will orchestrate and guide my life.

We tend, however, to divide our past into goods things to remember with gratitude and painful things to accept or forget. This way of thinking, which at first glance seems quite natural, prevents us from allowing our whole past to be the source from which we live our future. It locks us into a self-involved focus on our gain or comfort. It becomes a way to categorize and, in a way, control. Such an outlook becomes another attempt to avoid facing our suffering. Once we accept this division, we develop a mentality in which we hope to collect more good memories than bad memories, more things to be glad about than things to be resentful about, more things to celebrate than to complain about.

TURN MY MOURNING INTO DANCING

165

The Agony and the Ecstasy

Joy and sorrow are never separated. When our hearts rejoice at a spectacular view, we may miss our friends who cannot see it, and when we are overwhelmed with grief, we may discover what true friendship is all about. Joy is hidden in sorrow and sorrow in joy. If we try to avoid sorrow at all costs, we may never taste joy, and if we are suspicious of ecstasy, agony can never reach us either. Joy and sorrow are the parents of our spiritual growth.

BREAD FOR THE JOURNEY

Integrating the Shadow

It is very difficult for each of us to believe in Christ's words, "I did not come to call the virtuous, but sinners. . ." Perhaps no psychologist has stressed the need of self-acceptance as the way to self-realization so much as Carl Jung. For Jung, self-realization meant the integration of the shadow. It is the growing ability to allow the dark side of our personality to enter into our awareness and thus prevent a one-sided life in which only that which is presentable to the outside world is

166

considered as a real part of ourselves. To come to an inner unity, totality, and wholeness, every part of our self should be accepted and integrated. Christ represents the light in us. But Christ was crucified between two murderers and we cannot deny them, and certainly not the murderers who live in us.

INTIMACY

The Call of Compassion

It would be sad if we were to think about the compassionate life as a life of heroic self-denial. Compassion, as a downward movement towards solidarity instead of an upward movement towards popularity, does not require heroic gestures or a sensational turnaround. In fact, the compassionate life is mostly hidden in the ordinariness of everyday living. Even the lives of those whom we look up to for their examples of compassion show that the descending way towards the poor was, first of all, practiced through small gestures in everyday life.

The question that truly counts is not whether we imitate Mother Teresa, but whether we are open to the many little sufferings of those with whom we share our life. Are we willing to spend time with those who do not stimulate our curiosity? Do we listen to those who do not immediately attract us? Can we be compassionate to those whose suffering remains hidden from the eyes of the world? There is much hidden suffering: the suffering of the teenager who does not feel secure; the suffering of the husband and wife who feel that there is no love left between them; the suffering of the wealthy executive who thinks that people are more interested in his money than in him; the suffering of the gay man or woman who feels isolated from family and friends; the suffering of the countless people who lack caring friends, satisfying work, a peaceful home, a safe neighborhood; the suffering of the millions who feel lonely and wonder if life is worth living.

Once we look downward instead of upward on the ladder of life, we see the pain of people wherever we go, and we hear the call of compassion wherever we are.

True compassion always begins right where we are.

HERE AND NOW

Connection

One of the discoveries we make in prayer is that the closer we come to God, the closer we come to all our brothers and sisters in the human family. God is not a private God. The God who dwells in our inner sanctuary is also the God who dwells in the inner sanctuary of each human being. As we recognize God's presence in our own hearts, we can also recognize that presence in the hearts of others, because the God who has chosen us as a dwelling-place gives us the eyes to see the God who dwells in others. When we see only demons within ourselves, we can see only demons in others, but when we see God within ourselves, we can see God also in others.

This might sound rather theoretical but, when we pray, we will increasingly experience ourselves as part of a human family infinitely bound by God who created us to share, all of us, in the divine light.

HERE AND NOW

The Essence of Care

Real care is not ambiguous. Real care excludes indifference and is the opposite of apathy. The word "care" finds its roots in the Gothic "Kara" which means lament. The basic meaning of care is: to grieve, to experience sorrow, to cry out with. I am very much struck by this background of the word "care" because we tend to look at caring as an attitude of the strong towards the weak, of the powerful towards the powerless, of the "haves" toward the "have-nots." And, in fact, we feel quite uncomfortable with an invitation to enter into someone's pain before doing something about it.

Still, when we honestly ask ourselves which persons in our lives mean the most to us, we often find that it is those who, instead of giving much advice, solutions, or cures, have chosen rather to share our pain and touch our wounds with a gentle and tender hand. The friend who can be silent with us in a moment of despair or confusion, who can stay with us in an hour of grief and bereavement, who can tolerate not-knowing, not-curing, not-healing, and face with us the reality of our powerlessness, that is the friend who cares. . .

The friend who cares makes it clear that, whatever happens in the external world, being present to each other is what really matters. In fact, it matters more than pain, illness, or even death. It is remarkable how much consolation and hope we can receive from authors who, while offering no answers to life's questions, have the courage to articulate the situation of their lives in all honesty and directness. Kierkegaard, Sartre, Camus, Hammarskjöld and Merton—none of them have ever offered solutions. Yet many of us who have read their works have found new strength to pursue our own search. Their courage to enter so deeply into human suffering and to become present to their own pain gave them the power to speak healing words.

Therefore, to care means first of all to be present to each other. From experience you know that those who care for you become present to you. When they listen, they listen to you. When they speak, you know they speak to you. And when they ask questions, you know it is for your sake and not for their own. Their presence is a healing presence because they accept you on your terms, and they encourage you to take your own life seriously and to trust your own vocation.

OUT OF SOLITUDE

171

Caring for the Elderly

To care for the elderly means then that we allow the elderly to make us poor by inviting us to give up the illusion that we created our own life and that nothing and nobody can take it away from us. This poverty, which is an inner detachment, can make us free to receive the old stranger into our lives and make that person into a most intimate friend.

When care has made us poor by detaching us from the illusion of immortality, we can really become present to the elderly. We can then listen to what they say without worrying about how we answer. We can pay attention to what they have to offer without being concerned about what we can give. We can see what they are in themselves without wondering what we can be for them. When we have emptied ourselves of false occupations and preoccupations, we can offer free space to old strangers, where not only bread and wine but also the story of life can be shared.

AGING

Poverty of Mind

Someone who is filled with ideas, concepts, opinions, and convictions cannot be a good host. There is no inner space to listen, no openness to discover the gift of the other. It is not difficult to see how those "who know it all" can kill a conversation and prevent an interchange of ideas. Poverty of mind as a spiritual attitude is a growing willingness to recognize the incomprehensibility of the mystery of life. The more mature we become, the more we will be able to give up our inclination to grasp, catch, and comprehend the fullness of life and the more we will be ready to let life enter into us. . . .

A good host not only has to be poor in mind but also poor in heart. When our heart is filled with prejudices, worries, jealousies, there is little room for a stranger. In a fearful environment it is not easy to keep our hearts open to the wide range of human experiences. Real hospitality, however, is not exclusive but inclusive and creates space for a large variety of human experiences.

REACHING OUT

173

Watchfulness

This afternoon I worked a few hours alone in the river carrying heavy granite rocks to the bank and making piles. While doing this, I realized how difficult *"nepsis"*—the control of thoughts—about which I read this morning, really is. My thoughts not only wandered in all directions, but started to brood on many negative feelings, feelings of hostility towards people who had not given me the attention I wanted, feelings of jealousy towards people who received more than I, feelings of self-pity in regard to people who had not written, and many feelings of regret and guilt towards people with whom I had strained relationships. . . .

My reading about the spirituality of the desert has made me aware of the importance of *"nepsis." Nepsis* means mental sobriety, spiritual attention directed to God, watchfulness in keeping the bad thoughts away, and creating free space for prayer. While working with the rocks I repeated a few times the famous words of the old desert fathers: *"fuge, tace, et quiesce"* ("live in solitude, silence, and inner peace"), but only God knows how far I am, not only from this reality but even from this desire.

THE GENESEE DIARY

Waiting Calmly

During the Eucharist this morning we sang: "Thus says the Lord: By waiting and calm, you shall be saved. In quiet and trust lies your strength" (Isa. 30:15). That could be the program for my restless soul for the coming six months! I am impatient, restless, full of preoccupations, and easily suspicious. Maybe I just need to repeat this sentence very often and let it sink deep into my heart: "By waiting and calm, you shall be saved. In quiet and trust lies your strength." If these words could descend from my head into my heart and become part of my innermost self, I would be a converted man. "Lord Jesus Christ, Son of the Living God, have mercy on me, a sinner."

THE GENESEE DIARY

The Discipline of Forgiveness

I have often said, "I forgive you," but even as I said these words my heart remained angry or resentful. I still wanted to hear the story that tells me that I was right after all; I still wanted to hear apologies and excuses; I still wanted the

175

satisfaction of receiving some praise in return—if only the praise for being so forgiving!

But God's forgiveness is unconditional; it comes from a heart that does not demand anything for itself, a heart that is completely empty of self-seeking. It is this divine forgiveness that I have to practice in my daily life. It calls me to keep stepping over all my arguments that say forgiveness is unwise, unhealthy, and impractical. It challenges me to step over all my needs for gratitude and compliments. Finally, it demands of me that I step over that wounded part of my heart that feels hurt and wronged and that wants to stay in control and put a few conditions between me and the one whom I am asked to forgive.

This "stepping over" is the authentic discipline of forgiveness.

THE RETURN OF THE PRODIGAL SON

Self-Surrender

Love is an act of forgiving in which evil is converted to good and destruction into creation. In the truthful, tender, and disarmed encounter of love man is able to create. In this perspective it becomes clear that the sexual act is a religious act. Out of the total disarmament of man on his cross, exposing himself in his extreme vulnerability, the new man arises and manifests himself in freedom. Is it not exactly in this same act of self-surrender that we find our highest fulfilment which expresses itself in the new life we create? Religion and sexuality, which in the past have been so often described as opponents, merge into one and the same reality when they are seen as an expression of the total self-surrender in love.

INTIMACY

Spiritual Unity

Unity, intimacy, and integrity are the three spiritual qualities of the resurrected life. We are called to break through the boundaries of nationality, race, sexual orientation, age, and mental capacities and create a unity of love that allows the weakest among us to live well. We are called to go far beyond the places of lust, sexual need, and desire for physical union to a spiritual intimacy that involves body, mind, and heart. And we are called to let go of old ways of feeling good about ourselves and reach out to a new integration of the many facets of our humanity. These calls are calls to the resurrection. Caring for the body is preparing the body for the final resurrection while anticipating it in our daily lives through spiritual unity, intimacy, and integrity.

SABBATICAL JOURNEY

BEFRIENDING

DEATH

Desiring Death

Our life is a short opportunity to say "yes" to God's love. Our death is a full coming home to that love. Do we desire to come home? It seems that most of our efforts are aimed at delaying this homecoming as long as possible.

Writing to the Christians at Philippi, the apostle Paul shows a radically different attitude. He says: "I want to be gone and be with Christ, and this is by far the stronger desire—and yet for your sake to stay alive in this body is a more urgent need." Paul's deepest desire is to be completely united with God through Christ and that desire makes him look at death as a "positive gain." His other desire, however, is to stay alive in the body and fulfill, his mission. That will offer him an opportunity for fruitful work.

We are challenged once again to look at our lives from above. When, indeed, Jesus came to offer us full communion with God, by making us partakers of his death and resurrection, what else can we desire but to leave our mortal bodies and so reach the final goal of our existence? The only reason for staying in this valley of tears can be to continue the mission of Jesus who has sent us into the world as his Father sent him into the world. Looking from above, life is a short, often painful, mission, full of occasions to do fruitful work for God's kingdom, and death is the open door that leads into the hall of celebration where the king himself will serve us.

It all seems such an upside-down way of being! But it's the way of Jesus and the way for us to follow. There is nothing morbid about it. On the contrary, it's a joyful vision of life and death. As long as we are in the body, let us care well for our bodies so that we can bring the joy and peace of God's kingdom to those we meet on our journey. But when the time has come for our dying and death, let us rejoice that we can go home and be united with the One who calls us the beloved.

HERE AND NOW

Laying Bare

Death indeed simplifies; death does not tolerate endless shadings and nuances. Death lays bare what really matters, and in this way becomes your judge.

A LETTER OF CONSOLATION

Death as a Guest

Befriending death seems to be the basis of all other forms of befriending. I have a deep sense, hard to articulate, that if we could really befriend death we would be free people. So many of our doubts and hesitations, ambivalences, and insecurities are bound up with our deep-seated fear of death that our lives would be significantly different if we could relate to death as a familiar guest instead of a threatening stranger.

A LETTER OF CONSOLATION

Departing

This great mystery of God becoming God-with-us has very radical implications for the way we care for the dying. When God wants to die with and for us, we too have to die with and for each other. Tragically, however, we think about our death, first of all, as an event that separates us from others. It is departing. It is leaving others behind. It is the ending of precious relationships. It is the beginning of loneliness. Indeed, for us, death is primarily a separation and, even worse, an irreversible separation.

But Jesus died for us so that our death no longer has to be just separation. His death

184

opened the possibility for us to make our own death a way to union and communion. That's the radical turn that our faith allows us to make. But making that turn does not happen spontaneously. It requires care.

To care for the dying means to make them live their dying as a way to gather around them, not only those who come to visit, not only family and friends, but all of humanity, the living as well as the dead. When we say that it is not good for a human being to die alone, we touch a very deep mystery. It is the mystery that precisely in our death we need to be, more than ever, in communion with others. The passage of our life is the passage that, more than any other passage, needs to be made with others.

OUR GREATEST GIFT

Returning

Dying is returning home. But even though we have been told this many times by many people, we seldom desire to return home. We prefer to stay where we are. We know what we have; we do not know what we will get. Even the most appealing images of the afterlife cannot take away the fear of dying. We cling to life, even when our relationships are difficult, our economic circumstances harsh, and our health quite poor.

Still, Jesus came to take the sting out of death and to help us gradually realize that we don't have to be afraid of death, since death leads us to the place where the deepest desires of our hearts will be satisfied. It is not easy for us to truly believe that, but every little gesture of trust will bring us closer to this truth.

BREAD FOR THE JOURNEY

Overcoming Dark Forces

You are still afraid to die. That fear is connected with the fear that you are not loved. Your question "Do you love me?" and your question "Do I have to die?" are deeply connected. You asked these questions as a little child, and you are still asking them.

As you come to know that you are loved fully and unconditionally, you will also come to know that you do not have to fear death. Love is stronger than death; God's love was there for you before you were born and will be there for you after you have died.

Jesus has called you from the moment you were knitted together in your mother's womb. It is your vocation to receive and give love. But

186

from the very beginning you have experienced the forces of death. They attacked you all through your years of growing up. You have been faithful to your vocation even though you have often felt overwhelmed by darkness. You know now that these dark forces will have no final power over you. They seem overwhelming, but the victory is already won. It is the victory of Jesus, who has called you. He overcame for you the power of death so that you could live in freedom.

You have to claim that victory and not live as if death still controlled you. Your soul knows about the victory, but your mind and emotions have not fully accepted it. They go on struggling. In this respect you remain a person of little faith. Trust the victory and let your mind and emotions gradually be converted to the truth. You will experience new joy and new peace as you let that truth reach every part of your being. Don't forget: victory has been won, the powers of darkness no longer rule, love is stronger than death.

THE INNER VOICE OF LOVE

The Dying Hours

I know that many people live with the deep feeling that they have not done for those who have died what they wanted to do, and have no idea how to be healed from that lingering feeling of guilt. The dying have the unique opportunity to set free those whom they leave behind. During my "dying hours" my strongest feelings centered on my responsibility towards those who would mourn my death. Would they mourn in joy or with guilt, with gratitude or with remorse? Would they feel abandoned or set free? Some people had hurt me deeply, and some had been deeply hurt by me. My inner life had been shaped by theirs. I experienced a real temptation to hold on to them in anger or guilt. But I also knew that I could choose to let them go and surrender myself completely to the new life in Christ.

My deep desire to be united with God through Jesus did not spring from disdain for human relationships, but from an acute awareness of the truth that dying in Christ can be, indeed, my greatest gift to others. In this perspective, life is a long journey of preparation—of preparing oneself to truly die for others. It is a series of little deaths in which we are asked to release many forms of clinging and to move increasingly from needing others to living for them. The many passages we have to make as we grow from childhood to adolescence, from adolescence to adulthood, and from adulthood to old age offer ever-new opportunities to choose for ourselves or to choose for others. Questions keep coming up during these passages and confront us with hard choices: Do I desire power or service; do I want to be visible or remain hidden; do I strive for a successful career or do I keep following my vocation? In this sense, we can speak about life as a long process of dying to self, so that we will be able to live in the joy of God and give our lives completely to others.

BEYOND THE MIRROR

Saying Our Farewells

When we think about death, we often think about what will happen to us after we have died. But it is more important to think about what will happen to those we leave behind. The way we die has a deep and lasting effect on those who stay alive. It will be easier for our family and friends to remember us with joy and peace if we have said a grateful goodbye than if we die with bitter and disillusioned hearts.

The greatest gift we can offer our families and friends is the gift of gratitude. Gratitude sets them free to continue living without bitterness or self-recrimination.

BREAD FOR THE JOURNEY

On the Threshold

In the days following surgery, I began to discover what it meant that I had not died and would soon recover. . . . I had to face the simple fact that I had returned to a world from which I had been released. I was glad to be alive, but on a deeper level I was confused and wondered why it was that Jesus had not yet called me home. Yes, I was happy to be back among friends, but still I had to ask myself why it was better for me that I return to this "vale of tears." I was deeply grateful to know that I would be able to live longer with my family and community, but I also knew that living longer on this earth would mean more struggle, more pain, more anguish and more loneliness. Interiorly, it was not easy to receive the many expressions of gratitude for my healing. . . .

My main question became: "Why am I alive; why wasn't I found ready to enter into the house of God; why was I asked to return to a place where love is so ambiguous, where peace so hard to experience, and joy so deeply hidden in sorrow?" The question came to me in many ways, and I knew that I had to grow slowly into the answer. As I live my life in the years ahead of me, the question will be with me always, and I will never be allowed to let that question go completely. That question brings me to the heart of my vocation: to live with a burning desire to be with God and to be asked to keep proclaiming his love while missing its fulfillment.

BEYOND THE MIRROR

Fearing Death

You are so afraid of dying alone. Your deeply hidden memories of a fearful birth make you suspect that your death will be equally fearful. You want to be sure that you won't cling to your present existence but will have the inner freedom to let go and trust that something new will be given to you. You know that only someone who truly loves you can help you link this life with the next.

But maybe the death you fear is not simply the death at the end of your present life. Maybe the death at the end of your life won't be so fearful if you can die well now. Yes, the real death—the passing from time into eternity, from the transient beauty of this world to the lasting beauty of the next, from darkness into light—has to be made now. And you do not have to make it alone.

God has sent people to be very close to you as you gradually let go of the world that holds you captive. You must trust fully in their love. Then you will never feel completely alone. Even though no one can do it for you, you can make the lonely passage in the knowledge that you are surrounded by a safe love and that those who let you move away from them will be there to welcome you on the other side. The more you trust in the love of those God has sent to you, the more you will be able to lose your life and so gain it.

Success, notoriety, affection, future plans, entertainment, satisfying work, health, intellectual stimulation, emotional support—yes, even spiritual progress—none of these can be clung to as if they are essential for survival. Only as you let go of them can you discover the true freedom your heart most desires. That is dying, moving into the life beyond life. You must make that passage now, not just at the end of your earthly life. You cannot do it alone but, with the love of those who are being sent to you, you can

192

surrender your fear and let yourself be guided into the new land.

THE INNER VOICE OF LOVE

The Death of a Child

Many parents have to suffer the death of a child, at birth or at a very young age. There probably is no greater suffering than losing a child, since it so radically interferes with the desire of a father and mother to see their child grow up to be a beautiful, healthy, mature, and loving person. The great danger is that the death of a child will take away the parents' desire to live. It requires an enormous act of faith on the part of parents to truly believe that their children, however brief their lives, were given to them as gifts from God, to deepen and enrich their own lives.

Whenever parents can make that leap of faith, their children's short lives can become fruitful far beyond their expectations.

BREAD FOR THE JOURNEY

Dying Young

It is very hard to accept an early death. When friends who are seventy, eighty, or ninety years old die, we may be in deep grief and miss them very much, but we are grateful that they had long lives. But when a teenager, a young adult, or a person at the height of his or her career dies, we feel a protest rising from our hearts: "Why. . . Why so soon?. . . Why so young?. . . It is unfair."

But far more important than our quantity of years is the quality of our lives. Jesus died young. Saint Francis died young. Saint Thérèse of Lisieux died young. Martin Luther King, Jr. died young. We do not know how long we will live, but this not knowing calls us to live every day, every week, every year of our lives to its fullest potential.

BREAD FOR THE JOURNEY

Death's Solitude

A young Salvadorean woman stands in front of the casket that holds the body of her cruelly executed husband. She stands alone near the grave into which the casket will be lowered. Her eyes are closed, her arms folded across her body. She stands there barefoot, poor, empty. . . but very still. A deep quiet surrounds her. No shouts of grief, no cries of protest, no angry voices. It seems as if this young widow is

194

enveloped in a cloud of peace. All is over, all is quiet, all is well. Everything has been taken away from her, but the powers of greed and violence that robbed her of her lover can't reach that deep solitude of her heart. In the background stand her friends and neighbors. They form a protective circle around her. They honor and respect her solitude. Some are silent; some whisper words of consolation; some try to explain to each other what happened; some embrace and cry. But the woman stands there alone. She understands something that the powers of death cannot understand. There are a trust and confidence in her that are vastly more powerful than the weapons that killed her husband. The solitude of the living and the solitude of the dead greet each other.

. . .We have much to learn about God's resting in silence and solitude [on Holy Saturday]. The Salvadorean woman at her husband's graveside knew something about it. She participated in it and trusted that it would bear fruit in her. Even though we are surrounded by the racket of our world's preoccupations, we, like this woman, can rest in God's silence and solitude and let it bear fruit in us. It is a rest that has nothing to do with not being busy, although that might be a sign of it. The rest of God is a deep rest of the heart that can endure even as we are surrounded by the forces of death. It is the rest that offers us the hope that our hidden, often invisible existence, will become fruitful even though we cannot say how and when. It is the rest of faith that allows us to live on with a peaceful and joyful heart even when things are not getting better, even when painful situations are not resolved, even when revolutions and wars continue to disrupt the rhythm of our daily lives. This divine rest is known by all those who live their lives in the Spirit of Jesus. Their lives are not characterized by quietness, passivity, or resignation. On the contrary, they are marked by creative action for justice and peace. But that action comes forth from the rest of God in their hearts and is, therefore, free from obsession and compulsion, and rich in confidence and trust.

WALK WITH JESUS

Tears of Compassion

It might sound strange to consider grief a way to compassion. But it is. Grief asks me to allow the sins of the world—my own included—to pierce my heart and make me shed tears, many tears, for them. There is no compassion without many tears. If they can't be tears that stream from my eyes, they have to be at least tears that well up from my heart. When I consider the immense waywardness of God's children, our lust, our greed, our violence, our anger, our resentment, and when I look at them through the eyes of God's heart, I cannot but weep and cry out in grief. . .

This grieving is praying. There are so few mourners left in this world. But grief is the discipline of the heart that sees the sin of the world, and knows itself to be the sorrowful price of freedom without which love cannot bloom. I am beginning to see that much of praying is grieving. This grief is so deep not just because the human sin is so great, but also—and more so—because the divine love is so boundless. To become like the Father, whose only authority is compassion, I have to shed countless tears and so prepare my heart to receive anyone, whatever their journey has been, and forgive them from that heart.

THE RETURN OF THE PRODIGAL SON

The Grace of Grief

Mourning makes us poor; it powerfully reminds us of our smallness. But it is precisely here, in that pain or poverty or awkwardness, that the Dancer invites us to rise up and take the first steps. For in our suffering, not apart from it, Jesus enters our sadness, takes us by the hand, pulls us gently up to stand, and invites us to dance. We find the way to pray, as the psalmist did: "You have turned my mourning into dancing" (Psalm 30:11) because, at the center of our grief, we find the grace of God.

And as we dance, we realize that we don't have to stay on the little spot of our grief, but can step beyond it. We stop centering our lives on ourselves. We pull others along with us and invite them into the larger dance. We learn to make room for others—and the Gracious Other in our midst. And when we become present to God and God's people, we find our lives richer.

We come to know that all the world is our dance floor.

Our step grows lighter because God has called out others to dance as well.

T U R N M Y M O U R N I N G I N T O D A N C I N G

198

The Choreography of Death

"[There is] a time for mourning, a time for dancing" (Eccl. 3:4). But mourning and dancing are never fully separated. Their times do not necessarily follow each other. In fact, their times may become one time. Mourning may turn into dancing and dancing into mourning without showing a clear point where one ends and the other starts.

Often our grief allows us to choreograph our dance while our dance creates the space for our grief. We lose a beloved friend, and in the midst of our tears we discover an unknown joy. We celebrate a success, and in the midst of the party we feel deep sadness. Mourning and dancing, grief and laughter, sadness and gladness—they belong together as the sad-faced clown and the happy-faced clown who make us both cry and laugh. Let's trust that the beauty of our lives becomes visible where mourning and dancing touch each other.

BREAD FOR THE JOURNEY

Emotional Paralysis

When we lose a dear friend, someone we have loved deeply, we are left with a grief that can paralyze us emotionally for a long time. People we love become part of us. Our thinking, feeling and acting are codetermined by them. Our fathers, our mothers, our husbands, our wives, our lovers, our children, our friends. . . they are all living in our hearts. When they die a part of us dies too. That is what grief is all about: it is that slow and painful departure of someone who has become an intimate part of us. When Christmas, New Year, a birthday, or an anniversary comes, we feel deeply the absence of our beloved companion. We sometimes have to live a whole year or more before our hearts have fully said good-bye and the pain of our grief recedes. But as we let go of them they become part of our "members" and as we "re-member" them, they become guides on our spiritual journey.

Bread for the Journey

Remembrance

As we grow older we have more and more people to remember, people who have died before us. It is very important to remember those who have loved us and those we have loved. Remembering them means letting their spirits inspire us in our daily lives. They can become part of our spiritual communities and gently help us as we make decisions on our journeys. Parents, spouses, children, and friends, can become true spiritual companions after they have died. Sometimes they can become even more intimate to us after death than when they were with us in life.

Remembering the dead is choosing their ongoing companionship.

BREAD FOR THE JOURNEY

Bearing Fruit

. . .the great mystery is that all people who have lived with and in the Spirit of God participate through their death in the sending of the Spirit. Thus, God's Spirit of love continues to be sent to us and reveals how Jesus' death continues to bear fruit through all whose death is like his death, a death for others.

In this way, dying becomes the way to an everlasting fruitfulness. We touch here the most hope-giving aspect of our death. Our death may be the end of our success, our productivity, our fame, or our importance among people, but it is not the end of our fruitfulness. The opposite is true: the fruitfulness of our lives shows itself in its fullness only after we have died. We ourselves seldom see or experience our fruitfulness. Often we remain too preoccupied with our accomplishments and have no eye for the fruitfulness of what we live. But the beauty of life is that it bears fruit long after life itself has come to an end. Jesus says: "In all truth I tell you, unless a wheat grain falls into the earth and dies, it remains only a single grain; but if it dies, it yields a rich harvest" (John 12:24).

This is the mystery of Jesus' death and of the deaths of all who lived in his Spirit. Their lives yield fruit far beyond the limits of their short and often very localized existence.

OUR GREATEST GIFT

STAGE NINE

ARRIVING HOME

God's Search for Us

For most of my life I have struggled to find God, to know God, to love God. I have tried hard to follow the guidelines of the spiritual life—pray always, work for others, read the Scriptures—and to avoid the many temptations to dissipate myself. I have failed many times but always tried again, even when I was close to despair.

Now I wonder whether I have sufficiently realized that during all this time God has been trying to find me, to know me, and to love me. The question is not "How am I to find God?" but "How am I to let myself be found by him?" The question is not "How am I to know God?" but "How am I to let myself be known by God?" And, finally, the question is not "How am I to love God?" but "How am I to let myself be loved by God?" God is looking into the distance for me, trying to find me, and longing to bring me home. In all three parables which Jesus tells in response to the question of why he eats with sinners, he puts the emphasis on God's initiative. God is the shepherd who goes looking for his lost sheep. God is the woman who lights a lamp, sweeps out the house, and searches everywhere for her lost coin until she has found it. God is the father who watches and waits for his children, runs out to meet them, embraces them, pleads with them, begs and urges them to come home.

It might sound strange, but God wants to find me as much as, if not more than, I want to find God. Yes, God needs me as much as I need God. God is not the patriarch who stays home, doesn't move, and expects his children to come to him, apologize for their aberrant behavior, beg for forgiveness, and promise to do better. To the contrary, he leaves the house, ignoring his dignity by running towards them, pays no heed to apologies and promises of change, and brings them to the table richly prepared for them.

THE RETURN OF THE PRODIGAL SON

Beauty and Sadness

O Lord, your abundant love became visible today in the abundant beauty of nature. The sun covered the wide fields of the Genesee Valley. The sky was blue with pleasant cloud formations here and there; the trees bare but already suggesting the new season of green leaves; the fields still dark but full of promise. I looked from the ridge out over the valley and was overwhelmed by the stark beauty of the world in which I am living. I was filled with a sense of gratitude, but also with a sense of the shortness of life. When I saw the rich soil, I thought of Mother being buried in similar soil only a few months ago, and a strange sadness welled up within the experience of beauty. I can no longer tell her about what I saw, nor can I write her about the new spring, which she always welcomed with much joy. New life, new green leaves, new flowers, new what; but this spring she would not call my name and say, "Look here, look there!"

But you, O Lord, say "The grain of wheat must die to yield a rich harvest." I believe that her death will yield fruits. The day of your resurrection for which I am preparing myself is also a sign that there is hope for all who die. So, let my sadness be a sorrow that makes me more eager to follow you on the way to the cross and beyond it, to that Easter morning with its empty grave.

Let the beauty of the land deepen my joy as well as my sorrow, and thus draw me closer to you, my Lord and my Redeemer. Amen.

A Cry for Mercy

The Angel on the Road

Dear Lord, I will remain restless, tense, and dissatisfied until I can be totally at peace in your house. But I am still on the road, still journeying, still tired and weary, and still wondering if I will ever make it to the city on the hill. With Vincent van Gogh, I keep asking your angel, whom I meet on the road: "Does the road go uphill then all the way?" And the answer is: "Yes, to the very end." And I ask again: "And will the journey take all day long?" And the answer is: "From morning till night, my friend."

So I go on, Lord, tired, often frustrated, irritated, but always hopeful to reach one day the eternal city far away, resplendent in the evening sun.

There is no certainty that my life will be any easier in the years ahead, or that my heart will be any calmer. But there is the certainty that you are waiting for me and will welcome me home when I have persevered in my long journey to your house.

O Lord, give me courage, hope, and confidence. Amen.

A CRY FOR MERCY

Seeing the Sunset

There is an intimate relationship between joy and hope. While optimism makes us live as if someday soon things will go better for us, hope frees us from the need to predict the future and allows us to live in the present, with the deep trust that God will never leave us alone but will fulfill, the deepest desires of our heart. . . .

I remember once walking along the beach with a friend. We spoke intensely about our relationship, trying hard to explain ourselves to each other and to understand each other's feelings. We were so preoccupied with our mutual struggle that we didn't notice the magnificent sunset spreading a rich spectrum of color over the foam-capped waves breaking on the wide, silent beach.

Suddenly my friend exclaimed: "Look. . . look at the sun. . . look." He put his arm around my shoulder and together we gazed at the shimmering ball of fire vanishing gradually below the horizon of the wide ocean.

At that moment, we both knew about hope and joy.

HERE AND NOW

The Soul and God

Hesychastic prayer, which leads to that rest where the soul can dwell with God, is prayer of the heart. For us who are so mind-oriented it is of special importance to learn to pray with and from the heart. The Desert Fathers can show us the way. Although they do not offer any theory about prayer, their concrete stories and counsels offer the stones with which the later orthodox spiritual writers have built a very impressive spirituality. The spiritual writers of Mount Sinai, Mount Athos, and the *startsi* of nineteenth-century Russia are all anchored in the tradition of the desert. We find the best formulation of the prayer of the heart in the words of the Russian mystic Theophan the Recluse: "To pray is to descend with the mind into the heart, and there to stand before the face of the Lord, ever-present, all-seeing, within you." All through the centuries, this view of prayer has been central in hesychasm. Prayer is standing in the presence of God with the mind in the heart; that is, at that point of our being where there are no divisions or distinctions and where we are totally one. There God's Spirit dwells and there the great encounter takes place. There heart speaks to heart, because there we stand before the face of the Lord, all-seeing, within us.

T H E   W A Y   O F   T H E   H E A R T

A Murmuring Stream

The prayer of the heart ["Lord Jesus Christ, have mercy upon me"] . . . is indeed like a murmuring stream that continues underneath the many waves of every day and opens the possibility of living in the world without being of it and of reaching out to our God from the center of our solitude.

The prayer of the heart requires first of all that we make God our only thought. That means that we must dispel all distractions, concerns, worries, and preoccupations, and fill the mind with God alone. The Jesus prayer, or any other prayer form, is meant to be a help to gently empty our minds from all that is not God, and offer all the room to him and him alone. But that is not all. Our prayer becomes a prayer of the heart when we have localized in the center of our inner being the empty space in which our God-filled mind can descend and vanish, and where the distinctions between thinking and feeling, knowing and experiencing, ideas and emotions are transcended, and where God can become our host. "The Kingdom of God is within you" (Luke 17:21), Jesus said. The prayer of the heart takes these words seriously. When we empty our mind from all thoughts and our heart from all experiences, we can prepare in the center of our innermost being the home for the God who wants to dwell in us.

REACHING OUT

Indwelling

Discipline in the spiritual life means a gradual process of coming home to where we belong and listening there to the voice which desires our attention. It is the voice of the "first love." St John writes: "We are to love. . . because God loved us first" (1 John 4:19). It is this first love which offers us the intimate place where we can dwell in safety. The first love says: "You are loved long before other people can love you or you can love others. You are accepted long before you can accept others or receive their acceptance. You are safe long before you can offer or receive safety." Home is the place where that first love dwells and speaks gently to us. It requires discipline to come home and listen, especially when our fears are so noisy

213

that they keep driving us outside of ourselves. But when we grasp the truth that we already have a home, we may at last have the strength to unmask the illusions created by our fears and continue to return again and again and again.

Conversion, then, means coming home, and prayer is seeking our home where the Lord has built a home—in the intimacy of our own hearts. Prayer is the most concrete way to make our home in God.

IN THE HOUSE OF THE LORD

A Love Beyond Passion

When St. John says that fear is driven out by perfect love, he points to a love that comes from God, a divine love. He does not speak about human affection, psychological compatibility, mutual attraction, or deep interpersonal feelings. All of that has its value and beauty, but the perfect love about which St. John speaks embraces and transcends all feelings, emotions, and passions. The perfect love that drives out all fear is the divine love in which we are invited to participate. The home, the intimate place, the place of true belonging, is therefore not a place made by human hands. It is fashioned for us by God, who came to pitch his

214

tent among us, invite us to his place, and prepare a room for us in his own house.

IN THE HOUSE OF THE LORD

Pitching the Tent

Words for "home" are often used in the Old and New Testaments. The Psalms are filled with a yearning to dwell in the house of God, to take refuge under God's wings, and to find protection in God's holy temple; they praise God's holy place, God's wonderful tent, God's firm refuge. We might even say that "to dwell in God's house" summarizes all the aspirations expressed in these inspired prayers. It is therefore highly significant that St. John describes Jesus as the Word of God pitching his tent among us (John 1:14). He not only tells us that Jesus invites him and his brother Andrew to stay in his home (John 1:38–39), but he also shows how Jesus gradually reveals that he himself is the new temple (John 2:19) and the new refuge (Matthew 11:28). This is most fully expressed in the farewell address, where Jesus reveals himself as the new home: "Make your home in me, as I make mine in you" (John 15:4).

215

Jesus, in whom the fullness of God dwells, has become our home. By making his home in us he allows us to make our home in him. By entering into the intimacy of our innermost self, he offers us the opportunity to enter into his own intimacy with God. By choosing us as his preferred dwelling place, he invites us to choose him as our preferred dwelling place. This is the mystery of the incarnation. It is beautifully expressed during the Eucharist when the priest pours a little water into the wine, saying: "By the mingling of this water and wine, may we come to share in the divinity of him who humbled himself to share in our humanity." God's immeasurable love for us is expressed in this holy interchange. God so much desired to fulfill our deepest yearning for a home that God decided to build a home in us. Thus we can remain fully human and still have our home in God. In this new home the distinction between distance and closeness no longer exists. God, who is furthest away, came closest, by taking on our mortal humanity. Thus God overcomes all distinctions between "distant" and "close" and offers us an intimacy in which we can be most ourselves when most like God.

IN THE HOUSE OF THE LORD

A Place of Intimacy

When Jesus says: "Make your home in me as I make mine in you," he offers us an intimate place that we can truly call "home." Home is that place or space where we do not have to be afraid but can let go of our defenses and be free, free from worries, free from tensions, free from pressures. Home is where we can laugh and cry, embrace and dance, sleep long and dream quietly, eat, read, play, watch the fire, listen to music, and be with a friend. Home is where we can rest and be healed. The word "home" gathers a wide range of feelings and emotions up into one image, the image of a house where it is good to be: the house of love.

But in this world millions of people are homeless. Some are homeless because of their inner anguish, while others are homeless because they have been driven from their own towns and countries. In prisons, mental hospitals, refugee camps, in hidden-away city apartments, in nursing homes and overnight shelters, we get a glimpse of the homelessness of the people of our century.

This homelessness, however, is also visible in much less dramatic ways. While teaching university students who came from many different states and countries, I was struck by how lonely they were. For many years they live in small rooms, surrounded by strangers, far away from their families and friends. There is little privacy and even less community in their lives. Mostly, they have no contact with children or elderly people. Seldom do they belong to a welcoming neighborhood or a supportive faith community, and only very few know families where they can drop in anytime and feel at home. I have come to consider this situation in which thousands of young adults live as "normal," but when I examine it a little closer it is not hard to understand why so many feel rootless and even lost.

IN THE HOUSE OF THE LORD

The Eternal Now

Eternal life. Where is it? When is it? For a long time I have thought about eternal life as a life after all my birthdays have run out. For most of my years I have spoken about the eternal life as the "afterlife," as "life after death." But the older I become, the less interest my "afterlife" holds for me. Worrying not only about tomorrow, next year, and the next decade, but even about the next life, seems a false preoccupation. Wondering how things will be

218

for me after I die seems, for the most part, a distraction. When my clear goal is the eternal life, that life must be reachable right now, where I am, because eternal life is life in and with God, and God is where I am here and now.

The great mystery of the spiritual life—the life in God—is that we don't have to wait for it as something that will happen later. Jesus says: "Dwell in me as I dwell in you." It is this divine in-dwelling that is eternal life. It is the active presence of God at the center of my living—the movement of God's Spirit within us—that gives us the eternal life.

HERE AND NOW

So then you are no longer strangers and aliens, but you are citizens with the saints and also members of the household of God, built upon the foundation of the apostles and prophets, with Christ Jesus himself as the cornerstone. In him the whole structure is joined together and grows into a holy temple in the Lord; in whom you also are built together spiritually into a dwelling place for God. (Ephesians 2:19–22)